Classic Baking

Classic Baking

Rediscover much-loved classics

This edition published by Parragon Books Ltd in 2013 and distributed by

Parragon Inc.
440 Park Avenue South, 13th Floor
New York, NY 10016
www.parragon.com/lovefood

LOVE FOOD is an imprint of Parragon Books Ltd

ISBN 978-1-4723-2915-8

Printed in China

Designed by Sabine Vonderstein
New recipes by Angela Drake
Edited by Lin Thomas and Angela Drake

Notes for the Reader
This book uses standard kitchen measuring spoons and cups. All spoon and cup measurements are level unless otherwise indicated. Unless otherwise stated, milk is assumed to be whole, eggs are large, individual vegetables are medium, and pepper is freshly ground black pepper. Unless otherwise stated, all root vegetables should be washed in plain water and peeled prior to using.

Garnishes, decorations, and serving suggestions are all optional and not necessarily included in the recipe ingredients or method.

The times given are only an approximate guide. Preparation times differ according to the techniques used by different people and the cooking times may also vary from those given. Optional ingredients, variations, or serving suggestions have not been included in the time calculations.

Recipes using raw or very lightly cooked eggs should be avoided by infants, the elderly, pregnant women, convalescents, and anyone with a weakened immune system. Pregnant and breast-feeding women are advised to avoid eating peanuts and peanut products. People with nut allergies should be aware that some of the prepared ingredients used in the recipes in this book may contain nuts. Always check the packaging before use. Vegetarians should be aware that some of the prepared ingredients used in the recipes in this book may contain animal products. Always check the package before use.

Picture acknowledgements
The publisher would like to thank the following for permission to reproduce copyright material:

Getty Images: p.10 Alison Gootee; p.44 bottom image Shawna Lemay; p.45 and 146 top image Sharon Lapkin; p.115 top image Foodcollection RF; p.124 Ideas/Ed O'Riley; p. 145 and p.222 Studer-T. Veronika; p.147 Crystal Cartier; p.156 Anna Nemoy (Xaomena); p.172 top left image MargoLuc; p.173 Nichola Evans; p.182 top image Susie Adams; p.208 Michael Paul; p.223 Alexandra Grablewski; p.242 bottom right Karin Enge Vivar; p.243 Jill Ferry
iStock: additional images, ornaments and background note paper: p.2, 8, 9, 11, 36, 68, 72, 114, p.182 bottom right Emilie Duchesne, p.183 Svetlana Kolpakova
Sabine Vonderstein: flower images and postcard images; p.115 bottom right image; p.146 bottom right image; p.242 left images
Lace backgrounds: from the publication 'Lace', published by The Pepin Press, www.pepinpress.com

Contents

Introduction

Few forms of cooking are more satisfying than baking, and it's a tradition worth keeping in every home. While store-bought cakes may be immaculately presented, there's nothing like the smell of a beautiful cake baking in the oven. The home-baked flavor will almost certainly be far better than it's store-bought cousin, and you'll also know exactly what went into it!

With a wide variety of recipes to choose from, Classic Baking includes all the best traditional recipes, from timeless Chocolate Cake, Lemon Drizzle Loaf, and Carrot Cake to delicious Summer Fruit Tarts, Chocolate Chip Cookies, and Vanilla Cupcakes.

The basic skills of baking are easy to learn and you need little in the way of special equipment to make some impressive cakes and other baked goods. There are a few tips that are worth noting to be sure of success. Before you start, always preheat the oven to the correct temperature so it is ready to use once your cake is mixed. Read through the recipe, assemble all your ingredients, and measure everything before you start. Resist the temptation to open the oven door too often, and close it gently

instead of banging it shut. Always make sure your cake is completely cool before storing it.

Most important, remember that baking is a fun and rewarding pastime. The cakes and baked goods you make will be individual because they were made by you. So, why not revive the tradition of baking in your home today? You'll never be short of a home-baked treat to offer visitors when they drop by. All it needs is a little practice and you'll soon be turning out impressive cakes and baked goods for all the family to enjoy.

Happy baking!

Sheet Cakes

Almond Butter Cake

Makes 15

Ingredients

2½ cups white bread flour,
  plus extra for dusting
2¼ teaspoons active dry yeast
2 tablespoons granulated sugar
pinch of salt
½ cup milk
4 tablespoons salted butter,
  diced, plus extra for greasing
2 extra-large eggs, lightly beaten

For the Topping

1½ sticks unsalted butter,
  softened
¾ cup slivered almonds
¼ cup granulated sugar
¼ teaspoon ground cinnamon

1. Grease a 9 x 13-inch jellyroll pan. Put the flour into a large bowl and stir in the yeast, sugar, and salt. Make a well in the center.

2. Put the milk and butter into a small saucepan and heat gently until the butter has melted. Let cool for a few minutes, until the liquid is lukewarm.

3. Pour the milk mixture and beaten eggs into the bowl and mix well with a blunt knife to make a soft, sticky dough. Turn the dough onto a lightly floured surface and knead for 7–8 minutes, until smooth and elastic, adding a little more flour if the dough is sticky.

4. Roll the dough out to a rectangle almost as large as the prepared pan. Place the dough in the pan and push into the corners with your fingertips. Cover with lightly greased plastic wrap and let stand in a warm place for 45–55 minutes, or until the dough is puffy and has risen above the edges of the pan. Preheat the oven to 400°F.

5. For the topping, place the butter in a bowl and beat until pale and fluffy. Spoon into a pastry bag fitted with a small plain tip.

6. Using two fingers make deep indentations into the risen dough at even intervals (approximately two fingers' width apart). Pipe the butter into the indentations. Sprinkle with the slivered almonds. Mix together the sugar and cinnamon and sprinkle the mixture over the almonds.

7. Bake in the preheated oven for 12–15 minutes, then cover loosely with aluminum foil and bake for an additional 5–8 minutes, or until the cake is springy to the touch with a golden brown topping. Let cool in the pan for 10 minutes, then cut into slices. Serve warm or cold.

Coconut Bars

1. Preheat the oven to 350°F. Grease a 9-inch square cake pan and line the bottom with nonstick parchment paper.

2. Cream together the butter and granulated sugar until pale and fluffy, then gradually beat in the eggs. Stir in the orange rind, orange juice, and sour cream. Fold in the flour, baking powder, and dry coconut evenly using a metal spoon.

3. Spoon the batter into the prepared cake pan and level the surface. Bake in the preheated oven for 35–40 minutes, or until risen and firm to the touch.

4. Let cool for 10 minutes in the pan, then turn out and finish cooling on a wire rack.

5. For the frosting, lightly beat the egg white, just enough to break it up, and stir in the confectioners' sugar and dry coconut, adding enough orange juice to mix to a thick paste. Spread over the top of the cake, sprinkle with toasted shredded coconut, then let set before slicing into bars.

Makes 10

Ingredients
1 stick unsalted butter,
    plus extra for greasing
2 cups granulated sugar
2 eggs, beaten
finely grated rind of 1 orange
3 tablespoons orange juice
⅔ cup sour cream
1¼ cups all-purpose flour
1¼ teaspoons baking powder
1 cup dry unsweetened coconut
toasted shredded coconut,
    to decorate

For the Frosting
1 egg white
1⅔ cups confectioners' sugar
1 cup dry unsweetened coconut
about 1 tablespoon orange
    juice

Poppy Seed Streusel

Makes 12

Ingredients

1¾ cups all-purpose flour
1¾ teaspoons baking powder
¾ cup granulated sugar
3 eggs, lightly beaten
finely grated zest of ½ lemon
3½ cups sunflower oil
3 tablespoons milk
⅓ cup poppy seeds
confectioners' sugar, for dusting

For the Streusel Topping

1 cup all-purpose flour
1 teaspoon baking powder
5 tablespoons butter, at room
  temperature, diced, plus extra
  for greasing
⅓ cup granulated sugar

1. Preheat the oven to 325°F. Grease a 9 x 13-inch jellyroll pan.

2. Sift the flour and baking powder into a large bowl. Add the sugar, eggs, lemon zest, oil, and milk. Using an electric handheld mixer, beat together until thoroughly combined. Stir in the poppy seeds.

3. Spoon the batter into the prepared pan and gently spread out to the edges of the pan, using a spatula.

4. To make the streusel crumb topping, put the flour and baking powder into a bowl. Using your fingertips, rub the butter into the flour until the mixture resembles fine bread crumbs. Stir in the sugar. Spoon the streusel over the cake batter in an even layer, pressing down gently.

5. Bake in the preheated oven for 45–50 minutes, or until the top is light golden brown and a toothpick inserted into the cake comes out clean.

6. Let cool in the pan for 20 minutes, then transfer to a wire rack and let cool completely. Dust with confectioners' sugar and cut into squares to serve.

Poppy Seed Crumb Squares

1. Grease a 7 x 11-inch baking pan. Put the flour into a large bowl and stir in the dry yeast and sugar. Make a well in the center. Put the milk and butter into a small saucepan and heat gently until the butter has melted. Let cool for a few minutes, until the liquid is lukewarm.

2. Pour the milk mixture and beaten egg into the bowl and mix well with a blunt knife to make a soft, sticky dough. Turn the dough onto a lightly floured surface and knead for 5–6 minutes, until smooth and elastic, adding a little more flour if the dough is sticky. Roll out the dough to a rectangle almost as large as the prepared pan. Place the dough in the pan and push into the corners with your fingertips. Cover with lightly greased plastic wrap and let stand in a warm place for 1 hour 30 minutes, or until the dough is puffy and has almost doubled in size.

3. About 30 minutes before the dough is ready, make the filling; mix the cornstarch and ¼ cup of the milk in a heatproof bowl. Put the rest of the milk into a saucepan with the poppy seeds and sugar. Slowly bring to a boil, then whisk into the cornstarch mixture. Return the mixture to the saucepan and heat gently, stirring all the time until smooth and thick. Transfer to a bowl, stir in the raisins and lemon zest, and let cool for 20 minutes, stirring frequently to prevent a skin from forming. Preheat the oven to 350°F. Gently spread the poppy seed mixture in an even layer over the dough.

4. To make the crumb topping, put the flour and baking powder into a bowl and add the diced butter. Rub into the flour until the mixture resembles large bread crumbs. Stir in the sugar. Sprinkle the crumb topping over the poppy seed filling. Bake in the preheated oven for 30–35 minutes, or until the topping is golden brown. Let cool in the pan for 20 minutes, then transfer to a wire rack and let cool completely before slicing.

Makes 12

Ingredients

1½ cups white bread flour, plus extra for dusting
1 teaspoon active dry yeast
3 tablespoons granulated sugar
⅓ cup milk
2 tablespoons butter, plus extra for greasing
1 egg , lightly beaten

For the Filling

3 tablespoons cornstarch
1¼ cups milk
⅓ cup poppy seeds
½ cup granulated sugar
⅓ cup raisins
finely grated zest of ½ lemon

For the Crumb Topping

⅔ cup all-purpose flour
½ teaspoon baking powder
3 tablespoons butter, at room temperature, diced
3 tablespoons granulated sugar

Classic Crumb Bars

Makes 8

Ingredients

1¾ cups white bread flour,
   plus extra for dusting
1½ teaspoons active dry yeast
¼ cup granulated sugar
2 teaspoons finely grated
   lemon zest
⅔ cup milk
6 tablespoons butter, plus extra
   for greasing

For the Crumb Topping

1¼ cups all-purpose flour
5 tablespoons butter,
   at room temperature, diced
⅓ cup granulated sugar
confectioners' sugar, for dusting

1. Grease a 7 x 11-inch baking pan. Put the flour into a large bowl and stir in the dry yeast, sugar, and lemon zest. Make a well in the center.

2. Put the milk and 5 tablespoons of the butter into a small saucepan and heat gently until the butter has melted. Let cool for a few minutes until the liquid is lukewarm.

3. Pour the milk mixture into the bowl and mix well with a blunt knife to make a soft, sticky dough. Turn the dough onto a lightly floured surface and knead for 7–8 minutes, until smooth and elastic, adding a little more flour if the dough is sticky.

4. Put the dough into a clean bowl. Cover with greased plastic wrap and let stand in a warm place for 1–1¼ hours, or until the dough has almost doubled in size.

5. Turn out the dough onto a lightly floured surface and knead for 1 minute. Roll out to a rectangle almost as large as the prepared pan. Place the dough in the pan and push it into the corners with your fingertips. Cover with greased plastic wrap and let stand in a warm place for 25–30 minutes, or until the dough is puffy. Preheat the oven to 350°F.

6. To make the crumb topping, put the flour into a bowl and add the diced butter. Rub into the flour until the mixture resembles large bread crumbs. Stir in the sugar.

7. Melt the remaining butter and brush lightly all over the risen dough. Top with the crumb mixture. Bake in the preheated oven for 40–45 minutes, or until the crumb topping is golden brown. Let cool in the pan for 10 minutes, then transfer to a wire rack. Serve warm or cold, cut into bars and dusted with confectioners' sugar.

Chocolate Crumb Squares

1. Grease an 11 x 7-inch baking pan and line the bottom with parchment paper.

2. To make a vanilla pudding filling or custard, blend the vanilla pudding or custard powder and sugar with 2 tablespoons of the milk in a small heatproof bowl until smooth. Heat the rest of the milk in a small saucepan until almost boiling, then whisk into the pudding mixture.

3. Pour the mixture back into the pan and slowly bring to a boil, stirring all the time, to make a smooth and thick pudding. Pour the pudding into a clean bowl, cover the surface with a piece of plastic wrap (to prevent a skin from forming), and let stand until cold. Preheat the oven to 350°F.

4. To make the chocolate cake, put all the ingredients into a large bowl and, using an electric handheld mixer, beat together until smooth and creamy.

5. Spoon the batter into the prepared pan and gently level the surface with a spatula. Using a teaspoon, drop small dollops of pudding all over the top of the chocolate cake batter. Use a knife to gently swirl the pudding through the chocolate cake batter.

6. To make the crumb topping, put the flour, baking powder, and butter into a bowl and, using your fingertips, rub the butter into the flour to resemble coarse bread crumbs. Stir in the sugar and sprinkle the crumb topping over the top of the cake.

7. Bake in the preheated oven for 30-35 minutes, or until risen, golden brown, and a toothpick inserted into the cake comes out clean. Let cool completely in the pan, then dust with confectioners' sugar and cut into squares to serve.

Makes 12

Ingredients
1½ tablespoons instant vanilla
   pudding powder or custard
   powder
1½ tablespoons granulated
   sugar
1 cup milk

For the Chocolate Cake
1½ sticks butter, softened,
   plus extra for greasing
¾ cup granulated sugar
3 eggs
1¼ cups all-purpose flour,
   sifted
1¼ teaspoons baking powder
¼ cup unsweetened cocoa
   powder, sifted

For the Crumb Topping
⅓ cup all-purpose flour
¼ cup baking powder
3 tablespoons butter, at room
   temperature, diced
1½ tablespoons granulated
   sugar
confectioners' sugar, for dusting

Chocolate & Cherry Cream Slices

Makes 20

Ingredients

1⅓ cups all-purpose flour
½ teaspoon baking powder
1½ sticks butter, softened,
   plus extra for greasing
¾ cup granulated sugar
1 teaspoon vanilla extract
3 eggs, lightly beaten
3 tablespoons milk
1½ tablespoons unsweetened
   cocoa powder
2⅓ cups frozen pitted dark
   sweet cherries, defrosted
   and thoroughly drained

For the Filling

3 sheets of gelatin
⅓ cup water
1 cup reduced-fat cream cheese
3 tablespoons granulated sugar
1½ cups heavy cream,
   softly whipped

For the Chocolate Glaze

6 ounces semisweet chocolate,
   broken into pieces
2 tablespoons unsalted butter
2 teaspoons light corn syrup

1. Preheat the oven to 350°F. Grease a 13 x 9-inch baking pan (about 2 inches deep) and line the bottom and sides with parchment paper (making sure the paper comes about ½ inch above the edges of the pan).

2. Sift the all-purpose flour and baking powder into a large bowl. Add the butter, sugar, vanilla extract, eggs, and 1 tablespoon of the milk. Using a handheld electric mixer, beat together for 2–3 minutes, until the batter is thoroughly combined. Spoon half the batter into the prepared pan and gently level the surface with a spatula. Beat the remaining milk and cocoa powder into the rest of the batter and spread evenly over the top. Draw a knife through the two batters to create a swirled effect. Sprinkle with the cherries. Bake in the preheated oven for 30–35 minutes, or until just firm to the touch and a toothpick inserted into the cake comes out clean. Let cool completely in the pan.

3. To make the filling, put the gelatin sheets and water into a small saucepan and let soak for 10 minutes. Heat gently, stirring all the time, until the gelatin has completely dissolved. Let cool for 20 minutes. Put the cream cheese and sugar into a bowl and beat together until smooth. Fold in the softly whipped cream, then fold in the cooled gelatin liquid. Spread the filling over the top of the cake, leveling the surface with a spatula. Chill in the refrigerator for 2 hours, or until the filling is set.

4. To make the chocolate glaze, put the chocolate, butter, and syrup in a double boiler or a heatproof bowl set over a saucepan of simmering water and heat until melted. Remove from the heat and stir until smooth. Let the glaze stand for about 20 minutes, stirring occasionally until cooled but still spreadable. Using the paper as a guide, lift the cake out of the pan and place on a board. Using a warmed metal spatula, quickly spread the chocolate glaze in a thin and even layer over the filling. Use the prongs of a fork to draw wavy lines on the chocolate and cut into slices before the glaze sets.

Plum Crumb Slices

1. Preheat the oven to 350°F. Grease an 11 x 7-inch baking pan and line the bottom with parchment paper.

2. Put the butter, sugar, and almond extract into a large bowl and, using a handheld electric mixer, beat together until pale and creamy. Gradually beat in the eggs.

3. Sift the flour and baking powder over the butter mixture and fold in with the ground almonds until thoroughly combined. Spread the batter in an even layer in the prepared pan.

4. Arrange the plum quarters over the top of the batter, cut side facing up, pressing them down gently.

5. To make the crumb topping, put the flour, baking powder, and butter in a bowl and rub the butter into the flour until the mixture resembles coarse bread crumbs. Stir in the sugar.

6. Sprinkle the crumb mixture over the plums. Bake in the preheated oven for 40–50 minutes, or until a toothpick inserted into the cake comes out clean. Cover loosely with aluminum foil after 35 minutes to prevent the top from overbrowning.

7. Let the cake cool in the pan for 20 minutes, then transfer to a wire rack. Serve warm or cold, dusted with confectioners' sugar and cut into squares.

Makes 12

Ingredients
1 stick butter, softened, plus extra for greasing
½ cup granulated sugar
½ teaspoon almond extract
2 extra-large eggs, lightly beaten
1 cup all-purpose flour
1 teaspoon baking powder
¼ cup ground almonds (almond meal)
7 plums (about 1 pound), halved, pitted, and quartered

For the Crumb Topping
⅔ cup all-purpose flour
½ teaspoon baking powder
3 tablespoons butter, at room temperature, diced
2 tablespoons granulated sugar
confectioners' sugar, for dusting

Plum Squares

Makes 15

Ingredients
2¾ cups all-purpose flour,
   plus extra for dusting
2¾ teaspoons baking powder
2 sticks butter, at room
   temperature, diced, plus
   extra for greasing
¾ cup granulated sugar
2 eggs, lightly beaten
finely grated zest ½ lemon

For the Topping
⅔ cup reduced-fat cream cheese
1 egg, lightly beaten
2 tablespoons granulated sugar
1 tablespoon cornstarch
⅓ cup plum or damson
   preserves
confectioners' sugar, for dusting

1. Grease a 9 x 13-inch jellyroll pan and line the bottom with parchment paper. Preheat the oven to 350°F.

2. Sift the flour and baking powder into a large bowl and add the diced butter. Rub the butter into the flour until the mixture resembles coarse bread crumbs, then stir in the sugar. Remove about one-sixth of the crumb mixture and set aside in a bowl.

3. Stir the beaten eggs and lemon zest into the remaining crumb mixture and mix with a blunt knife until beginning to clump together. Gather into a soft dough with your hands. Press the dough into the bottom of the prepared pan, using the palms of your hands (dusted with a little flour if the mixture is too sticky).

4. To make the topping, put the cream cheese into a bowl and gradually beat in the egg, sugar, and cornstarch until smooth. Spread over the dough.

5. Drop small spoonfuls of the preserves all over the cream cheese mixture, then top with the reserved crumb topping.

6. Bake in the preheated oven for 35–40 minutes, or until just golden brown and set. Let cool in the pan for 20 minutes, then transfer to a wire rack to cool completely. Dust with confectioners' sugar, then cut into squares to serve.

Apple Strudels

1. Preheat the oven to 400°F. Lightly grease a large baking sheet.

2. To make the filling, put the raisins into a small bowl and add the hot rum or apple juice. Let soak for 15 minutes.

3. Put the apple slices into a large bowl and toss in the lemon juice and vanilla extract. Add the sugar, cinnamon, slivered almonds, and soaked raisins and mix together gently.

4. In a separate bowl, beat together the cream cheese with half the light cream and the egg yolks until smooth. Add the apple mixture to this bowl and stir gently to mix.

5. Take one sheet of the phyllo dough and brush lightly with melted butter, then sprinkle with some of the bread crumbs. Spoon one-sixth of the apple filling onto the lower third of the sheet. Gently roll up the pastry to enclose the filling and pinch both the pastry ends together tightly.

6. Place, seam side down, on the prepared baking sheet and repeat with the rest of the sheets of phyllo pastry and filling to make six strudels in total. Brush the top of the strudels with the rest of the cream. Bake in the preheated oven for 25–30 minutes, until light golden brown. Serve warm, dusted with confectioners' sugar.

Makes 6

Ingredients

3 tablespoons raisins
1 tablespoon hot rum or
  apple juice
6 small Pippin or other sweet
  crisp apples, peeled, cored,
  and thinly sliced
1 tablespoon lemon juice
1 teaspoon vanilla extract
½ cup granulated sugar
½ teaspoon ground cinnamon
3 tablespoons slivered almonds,
  lightly toasted
½ cup reduced-fat cream cheese
¼ cup light cream
2 egg yolks
6 sheets phyllo dough
3 tablespoons butter, melted,
  plus extra for greasing
3 tablespoons fresh white
  bread crumbs
confectioners' sugar, for dusting

Chocolate & Cinnamon Brownies

Makes 16

Ingredients

4 ounces semisweet chocolate,
 broken into pieces
1¾ sticks butter, plus extra
 for greasing
1 cup pecan halves
1¼ cups granulated sugar
4 eggs, beaten
1¾ cups all-purpose flour
2 teaspoons ground cinnamon
2 ounces white chocolate,
 broken into pieces
2 tablespoons milk
1 cup confectioners' sugar

1. Preheat the oven to 350°F. Grease a shallow 9-inch square cake pan.

2. Melt the semisweet chocolate and 1½ sticks of the butter in a double boiler or a heatproof bowl set over a saucepan of gently simmering water. Remove from the heat and let cool slightly.

3. Set 16 pecan halves to one side for decoration and chop the rest. Beat together the granulated sugar and eggs until thick and creamy, then fold in the chocolate mixture, flour, cinnamon, and chopped pecans.

4. Transfer the batter to the prepared pan and bake in the preheated oven for 35–40 minutes, or until just firm to the touch. Let cool in the pan.

5. Melt the remaining butter and white chocolate in a double boiler or heatproof bowl set over a saucepan of gently simmering water. Remove from the heat and beat in the milk and confectioners' sugar. Spread this mixture over the cooled brownies. Let set for 30 minutes, then cut into 16 squares and top each square with a pecan half.

Fudge Blondies

1. Preheat the oven to 350°F. Grease a shallow 8-inch square cake pan and line with parchment paper.

2. Place the butter and brown sugar in a large bowl and beat together until pale and creamy. Gradually beat in the eggs and vanilla extract. Sift the flour and baking powder into the mixture and beat together until well mixed.

3. Add the fudge and chopped nuts and stir together until combined. Spoon the batter into the prepared pan and smooth the surface.

4. Bake in the preheated oven for 40–45 minutes, or until risen and golden brown. Let cool in the pan, then dust with sifted confectioners' sugar to decorate and cut into squares.

Makes 9

Ingredients

1 stick butter, softened, plus extra for greasing
1 cup firmly packed light brown sugar
2 extra-large eggs, beaten
1 teaspoon vanilla extract
2 cups all-purpose flour
1 teaspoon baking powder
4 ounces soft fudge, chopped into small pieces
½ cup coarsely chopped macadamia nuts
confectioners' sugar, for dusting

Double Chocolate Pecan Blondies

Makes 12

Ingredients

- 8 ounces white chocolate, broken into pieces
- 3 tablespoons butter, plus extra for greasing
- 6 ounces semisweet chocolate
- 2 extra-large eggs, beaten
- ⅓ cup granulated sugar
- 1 cup all-purpose flour
- 1 teaspoon baking powder
- 1 cup coarsely chopped pecans

1. Preheat the oven to 350°F. Grease a shallow 8-inch square baking pan and line it with parchment paper.

2. Put 3 ounces of the white chocolate and the butter into a double boiler or a heatproof bowl set over a saucepan of gently simmering water and heat, stirring occasionally, until melted and smooth. Meanwhile, coarsely chop the remaining white and semisweet chocolate.

3. Beat together the eggs and sugar in a large bowl, then stir in the melted chocolate mixture. Sift the flour and baking powder over the top. Add the chopped chocolate and pecans. Mix well.

4. Spoon the batter into the prepared pan and smooth the surface. Bake in the preheated oven for 35–40 minutes, or until golden brown and just firm to the touch in the center. Let cool in the pan until completely cooled and the chocolate chunks inside have set, then turn out and cut into pieces.

Chocolate & Cherry Brownies

Makes 12

Ingredients

- 6 ounces semisweet chocolate, broken into pieces
- 1½ sticks butter, plus extra for greasing
- 1 cup granulated sugar
- 3 extra-large eggs, beaten
- 1 teaspoon vanilla extract
- 1 cup all-purpose flour
- 1 teaspoon baking powder
- 1 cup pitted fresh sweet cherries
- 3 ounces white chocolate, chopped

1. Preheat the oven to 350°F. Grease a shallow 9½ x 8-inch cake pan and line with parchment paper.

2. Put the semisweet chocolate and butter into a double boiler or a large, heatproof bowl set over a saucepan of simmering water and heat until melted. Remove from the heat and let cool for 5 minutes.

3. Beat the sugar, eggs, and vanilla extract into the chocolate mixture. Sift in the flour and baking powder and fold in gently. Pour the mixture into the prepared pan. Sprinkle the cherries over the top, followed by the chopped white chocolate.

4. Bake in the preheated oven for 30 minutes. Loosely cover the tops of the brownies with aluminum foil and bake for an additional 15–20 minutes, or until just firm to the touch. Let cool in the pan, then cut into pieces.

Apple Crumb Squares

Makes 15

Ingredients

1½ sticks butter, softened,
    plus extra for greasing
⅔ cup granulated sugar
1 teaspoon vanilla extract
2 extra-large eggs, lightly
    beaten
1⅓ cups all-purpose flour
1¼ teaspoons baking powder
3 tablespoons milk
finely grated zest of ½ lemon
4 Pippin or other sweet crisp
    apples (about 1 pound),
    peeled, cored, and
     thinly sliced
1 tablespoon lemon juice

For the Crumb Topping

1 cup all-purpose flour
1 teaspoon baking powder
6 tablespoons butter
¼ cup granulated sugar
¼ cup ground almonds
    (almond meal)
confectioners' sugar, for dusting

1. Preheat the oven to 325°F. Grease a 13 x 9-inch baking pan (about 2 inches deep) and line the bottom with parchment paper.

2. Put the butter, sugar, and vanilla extract into a large bowl and, using a handheld electric mixer, beat together until pale and creamy. Gradually beat in the eggs.

3. Sift the flour and baking powder over the butter mixture and fold in with the milk and lemon zest until thoroughly combined. Spread the batter in an even layer in the prepared pan.

4. Toss the apples in the lemon juice and arrange over the top of the batter.

5. To make the crumb topping, put the flour, baking powder, and butter into a bowl and rub the butter into the flour until the mixture resembles coarse bread crumbs. Stir in the sugar and ground almonds.

6. Sprinkle the crumb mixture over the apples. Bake in the preheated oven for 45–50 minutes, or until the topping is golden brown and a toothpick inserted into the cake comes out clean.

7. Let the cake cool in the pan. Serve warm or cold, dusted with confectioners' sugar and cut into squares.

Pear Squares

1. Preheat the oven to 350°F. Grease an 11 x 7-inch baking pan and line the bottom with parchment paper.

2. Put the butter, sugar, vanilla extract, and lemon zest into a large bowl and, using an electric handheld mixer, beat together until pale and creamy. Gradually beat in the eggs. Sift the flour and baking powder over the butter mixture and fold in with the milk.

3. Spoon the batter into the prepared pan and gently level with a spatula. Arrange the sliced pears on top of the batter, pressing them down gently. Sprinkle with the raisins and almonds.

4. Bake in the preheated oven for 45–50 minutes, or until risen, golden brown, and firm to the touch.

5. Brush the top of the hot cake liberally with the strained, warmed apricot preserves. Let the cake cool in the pan for 20 minutes, then transfer to a wire rack to cool completely. Dust with confectioners' sugar, then cut into squares to serve.

Makes 15

Ingredients
2 sticks butter, softened,
*   plus extra for greasing*
1 cup granulated sugar
1 teaspoon vanilla extract
finely grated zest of ½ lemon
4 eggs, lightly beaten
1¾ cups all-purpose flour
1¾ teaspoons baking powder
3 tablespoons milk
3 pears peeled, cored and sliced
2 tablespoons raisins
2 tablespoons slivered almonds
2 tablespoons apricot preserves,
*   warmed and strained*
confectioners' sugar, for dusting

Chocolate & Pear Squares

Makes 20

Ingredients

1⅓ cups all-purpose flour
1¾ teaspoons baking powder
2 tablespoons unsweetened
  cocoa powder
1½ sticks butter, softened,
  plus extra for greasing
¾ cup granulated sugar
1 teaspoon vanilla extract
3 eggs
2 ounces semisweet chocolate,
  melted
1 (15-ounce) can pears halves
  in natural juice, drained,
  reserving ½ cup of the juice

For the Topping

3 sheets of gelatin
1¾ cups heavy cream
¼ cup confectioners' sugar,
  sifted
1¼ cups sour cream

To Decorate

1 tablespoon confectioners'
  sugar
1 tablespoon unsweetened
  cocoa powder

1. Preheat the oven to 350°F. Grease a 13-inch x 9-inch baking pan (about 2 inches deep) and line the bottom and sides with parchment paper (making sure the paper comes about ½ inch above the edges of the pan).

2. Sift the all-purpose flour, baking powder, and cocoa into a large bowl. Add the butter, sugar, vanilla extract, and eggs. Using a handheld electric mixer, beat together for 2–3 minutes, until the batter is thoroughly combined. Fold in the melted chocolate. Spoon the batter into the prepared pan and gently level the surface with a spatula. Thinly slice the drained pear halves and arrange over the chocolate batter, pressing down gently.

3. Bake in the preheated oven for 30–35 minutes, or until just firm to the touch and a toothpick inserted into the cake comes out clean. Let cool completely in the pan. To make the topping, put the gelatin sheets into a shallow bowl and cover with cold water. Let soak for 5 minutes, until soft. Remove the sheets from the water and squeeze out the excess liquid. Put the sheets in a small saucepan with the reserved pear juice. Heat gently until the gelatin has completely dissolved. Let cool for 15 minutes.

4. Whip together the cream and confectioners' sugar in a large bowl until holding firm peaks. Fold in the sour cream, then gradually beat in the cooled gelatin liquid. Spread the cream mixture over the top of the cold cake and level the surface. Chill in the refrigerator for 2 hours, or until the cream topping is set.

5. To decorate, carefully lift the cake out of the pan, using the lining paper to help you. Lay thin strips of paper in a random pattern over the topping. Mix together the confectioners' sugar and cocoa powder and sift over the strips of paper. Lift the paper strips away and cut the cake into squares.

Tea for two
&
a slice of cake

Rhubarb Meringue Squares

1. Preheat the oven to 350°F. Grease a 9 x 13-inch jellyroll pan and line with parchment paper.

2. Sift the flour into a large bowl and add the diced butter. Rub the butter into the flour until it resembles coarse bread crumbs. Stir in the sugar and egg and mix with a blunt knife until beginning to clump together.

3. Turn the crumbly dough into the prepared pan and, using lightly floured hands, press out firmly in an even layer in the bottom of the pan. Smooth level with the back of a spoon. Bake in the preheated oven for 15 minutes, until pale golden brown.

4. To prepare the filling, place the chopped rhubarb in a bowl and stir in the sugar and raspberries. Spread over the baked cake and return to the oven for 30 minutes. Remove from the oven and increase the oven temperature to 400°F.

5. To make the meringue, put the egg whites into a bowl and beat until holding stiff peaks. Gradually beat in the sugar, one spoonful at a time, until you have a firm glossy meringue.

6. Spread the meringue over the top of the fruit and right to the edges of the pan. Return the pan to the oven and bake for an additional 5-10 minutes, or until the top of the meringue is golden brown. Serve warm or cold, cut into squares straight from the pan, dusted with confectioners' sugar.

Makes 15

Ingredients

1¾ cups all-purpose flour,
 plus extra for dusting
1¼ stick butter, at room
 temperature, diced,
 plus extra for greasing
⅓ cup granulated sugar
1 extra-large egg, lightly beaten

For the Filling

4 cups ¾-inch young pink
 rhubarb pieces
¼ cup granulated sugar
1 cup frozen raspberries

For the Meringue

3 extra-large egg whites
⅔ cup superfine sugar or
 granulated sugar
confectioners' sugar, for dusting

Caramel Squares

Makes 16

Ingredients

1 stick butter, softened,
   plus extra for greasing
¼ cup granulated sugar
1⅓ cups all-purpose flour
½ cup ground almonds
   (almond meal)

For the Topping

1½ sticks butter
⅔ cup granulated sugar
3 tablespoons light corn syrup
1 (14-ounce) can condensed
   milk
¼ teaspoon sea salt crystals
3 ounces semisweet chocolate,
   melted

1. Preheat the oven to 350°F. Grease a shallow 8-inch square cake pan.

2. Put the butter and sugar into a bowl and beat together until pale and creamy. Sift in the flour and add the ground almonds. Use clean hands to mix and knead to a crumbly dough. Press into the bottom of the prepared pan and prick the surface all over with a fork. Bake in the preheated oven for 15 minutes, or until pale golden brown. Let cool.

3. To make the topping, put the butter, sugar, corn syrup, and condensed milk into a saucepan over low heat and heat gently until the sugar has dissolved. Increase the heat to medium, bring to a boil, then simmer for 6–8 minutes, stirring constantly, until the mixture becomes thick. Stir in half the salt, then quickly pour the caramel over the shortbread. Sprinkle with the remaining salt.

4. Spoon the chocolate into a paper pastry bag and snip off the end. Pipe the chocolate over the caramel and swirl with the tip of a knife. Let cool, then chill for 2 hours, or until firm. Cut into 16 squares.

Coconut Squares

1. Preheat the oven to 350°F. Grease a shallow 9-inch square cake pan.

2. Beat together the butter and sugar in a large bowl until fluffy. Beat in the egg yolk, then sift in the flour and mix to a soft dough. Knead lightly, then press into the bottom of the prepared pan. Prick all over with a fork and bake in the preheated oven for 20–25 minutes, or until pale golden brown.

3. To make the topping, put the egg whites into a large bowl and beat until holding stiff peaks. Gradually beat in the sugar to make a firm, glossy meringue. Fold in ½ cup of the coconut. Spread the jelly or preserves over the cooked cake in the pan, then spoon the meringue over the jelly. Sprinkle with the remaining coconut.

4. Return to the oven for 15–20 minutes, or until the top of the meringue is crisp and golden brown. Let cool in the pan, then dust with unsweetened cocoa powder, if using, and cut into nine squares.

Makes 9

Ingredients
1¼ sticks butter, softened,
   plus extra for greasing
⅓ cup granulated sugar
1 extra-large egg yolk
1⅔ cups all-purpose flour
⅓ cup seedless raspberry jelly
   or preserves
unsweetened cocoa powder,
   to dust (optional)

For the Coconut Topping
2 extra-large egg whites
⅔ cup superfine sugar or
   granulated sugar
⅔ cup dry unsweetened coconut

Raspberry Mousse Squares

Makes 12

Ingredients
1 stick butter, softened,
  plus extra for greasing
⅔ cup granulated sugar
1 teaspoon vanilla extract
2 eggs, lightly beaten
1 cup all-purpose flour
1 teaspoon baking powder
1 tablespoon milk

For the Mousse
4 sheets of gelatin
3⅓ cups fresh raspberries
(about 1 pound), plus extra
  for decoration
⅓ cup granulated sugar
1¼ cups heavy cream
2 tablespoons slivered almonds,
  toasted
confectioners' sugar, for dusting

1. Preheat the oven to 350°F. Grease an 11 x 7-inch baking pan and line the bottom with parchment paper.

2. Put the butter, sugar, and vanilla extract into a large bowl and, using a handheld electric mixer, beat together until pale and creamy. Gradually beat in the eggs.

3. Sift the flour and baking powder over the butter mixture and fold in with the milk until thoroughly combined. Spread the batter in an even layer in the prepared pan.

4. Bake in the preheated oven for 18–20 minutes, or until risen and golden brown and just firm to the touch. Let cool in the pan for 10 minutes, then turn out onto a wire rack, peel off the lining paper, and let cool completely.

5. To make the mousse, soak the gelatin sheets in a bowl of cold water for 10 minutes, until soft. Press 1 cup of the raspberries through a fine-mesh strainer to make a smooth puree.

6. Place the puree in a small saucepan with the sugar. Remove the gelatin sheets from the water and squeeze out the excess liquid. Add to the puree and heat gently, stirring all the time, until the gelatin has dissolved. Let cool for 15 minutes.

7. Pour the cream into a large bowl and whip until holding firm peaks. Gradually beat in the puree. Lightly crush the remaining raspberries with a fork and fold into the cream mixture.

8. Return the cold cake to the baking pan. Spread the raspberry mixture over the top of the cake in an even layer. Chill in the refrigerator for 2–3 hours, or until set. Decorate with slivered almonds and raspberries, and dust lightly with confectioners' sugar. Cut into squares to serve.

Raspberry Sponge Cake Roll

1. Preheat the oven to 350°F. Grease and line a 9 x 13-inch jellyroll pan with the paper ½ inch above the rim. Lay a sheet of parchment paper on the work surface and sprinkle with granulated sugar.

2. Sift the flour and baking powder into a large bowl and add the butter, sugar, eggs, and vanilla extract. Beat well until the mixture is smooth, then beat in the milk.

3. Spoon the batter into the prepared pan and smooth into the corners with a spatula. Bake in the preheated oven for 15–20 minutes, or until risen, firm, and golden brown.

4. When cooked, turn out the cake onto the sugared parchment paper and spread with the preserves. Roll up the cake firmly from one short side to enclose the perserves, keeping the paper around the outside to hold it in place.

5. Lift onto a wire rack to cool, removing the paper when firm. Sprinkle with granulated sugar, cut into slices, and serve.

Serves 8

Ingredients

oil or melted butter,
  for greasing
1¼ cups all-purpose flour
1½ teaspoons baking powder
1½ sticks unsalted butter,
  softened
¾ cup granulated sugar, plus
  extra for sprinkling
3 eggs, beaten
1 teaspoon vanilla extract
2 tablespoons milk
½ cup raspberry preserves,
  warmed

Blueberry Sheet Cake

Makes 12

Ingredients

2 cups all-purpose flour,
    plus extra for dusting
1 teaspoon baking powder
1½ sticks butter, at room
    temperature, diced,
    plus extra for greasing
⅓ cup granulated sugar
1 egg, lightly beaten

For the Topping

2 eggs
⅔ cup heavy cream
½ cup granulated sugar
¼ cup blueberry preserves
1⅓ cups fresh blueberries

1. Preheat the oven to 350°F. Grease a 9 x 13-inch jellyroll pan and line with parchment paper.

2. Sift the flour and baking powder into a large bowl and add the diced butter. Rub the butter into the flour until it resembles coarse bread crumbs. Stir in the sugar and egg and mix with a blunt knife until beginning to clump together.

3. Gather the dough together and knead lightly on a floured surface. Press the dough out in an even layer in the bottom of the pan, using floured hands. Prick all over with the prongs of a fork.

4. Bake in the preheated oven for 15 minutes, until pale golden brown. Remove from the oven and let cool. Keep the oven on.

5. To make the topping, put the eggs, cream, and sugar into a bowl and beat together until smooth.

6. Spread the perserves over the partly baked cake, then gently spoon the eggs and cream mixture over the top. Sprinkle with the blueberries and return to the oven for 25 minutes, or until the topping is set and pale golden brown. Serve warm or cold, sliced, from the pan.

Red Currant Crumb Squares

1. Preheat the oven to 350°F. Grease an 11 x 7-inch baking pan and line the bottom with parchment paper.

2. Sift the flour and baking powder into a large bowl and add the diced butter. Rub the butter into the flour until the mixture resembles coarse bread crumbs. Stir in the sugar and make a well in the center. Add the egg and milk and mix with a blunt knife to a soft, crumbly dough. Knead lightly on a floured surface.

3. Use floured hands to press the dough out evenly in the bottom of the prepared pan. Spread the red currants on top.

4. To make the crumb topping, place the flour, baking powder, and butter in a bowl and rub the butter into the flour until the mixture resembles coarse bread crumbs. Stir in the sugar.

5. Sprinkle the crumb mixture over the red currants. Bake in the preheated oven for 40–45 minutes, or until a toothpick inserted into the cake comes out clean.

6. Let the cake cool in the pan for 20 minutes, then transfer to a wire rack. Serve warm or cold, dusted with confectioners' sugar, cut into squares and decorated with red currant sprigs, if desired.

Makes 12

Ingredients
1¾ cups all-purpose flour, plus extra for dusting
1¾ teaspoons baking powder
1 stick butter, at room temperature, diced, plus extra for greasing
½ cup granulated sugar
1 egg, lightly beaten
1 tablespoon milk
2⅔ cups fresh red currants or blueberries, sprigs removed

For the Crumb Topping
⅔ cup all-purpose flour
½ teaspoon baking powder
3 tablespoons butter, at room temperature, diced
¼ cup granulated sugar
confectioners' sugar, for dusting
red currant sprigs, for decoration (optional)

Gooseberry Squares

Makes 15

Ingredients
butter, for greasing
1½ cups white bread flour,
  plus extra for dusting
1 teaspoon active dry yeast
2 tablespoons granulated sugar
½ cup lukewarm milk
1 egg, lightly beaten

For the Filling
1½ cups reduced-fat cream
  cheese
2 tablespoons cornstarch
⅓ cup granulated sugar
2 eggs, lightly beaten
finely grated zest of ½ lemon
1½ cups small fresh
  gooseberries, trimmed,
  or 1 cup canned gooseberries

For the Crumb Topping
⅔ cup all-purpose flour
3 tablespoons butter, at room
  temperature, diced
¼ cup granulated sugar
finely grated zest of ½ lemon
confectioners' sugar, for dusting

1. Grease a 9 x 13-inch jellyroll pan. Put the flour into a large bowl and stir in the dry yeast and sugar. Make a well in the center.

2. Pour the milk and egg into the well and mix with a blunt knife to make a soft sticky dough. Turn the dough onto a lightly floured surface and knead for 7–8 minutes, until smooth and elastic, adding a little more flour if the dough is sticky.

3. Put the dough into a clean bowl. Cover with greased plastic wrap and let stand in a warm place for about 1¼ hours, until the dough has almost doubled in size.

4. Turn out the dough onto a lightly floured surface and knead for 1 minute. Roll out to a rectangle almost as large as the prepared pan. Put the dough into the pan and push it into the corners with your fingertips. Cover with greased plastic wrap and let stand in a warm place for 30 minutes, until puffy. Preheat the oven to 350°F.

5. To make the filling, put the cream cheese into a large bowl and beat in the cornstarch, sugar, eggs, and lemon zest until smooth.

6. Spread the filling over the top of the dough then sprinkle with the gooseberries, pressing them down gently.

7. To make the crumb topping, put the flour and butter into a bowl and, using your fingertips, rub the butter into the flour until it resembles coarse bread crumbs. Stir in the granulated sugar and lemon zest. Sprinkle the topping over the filling.

8. Bake in the preheated oven for 55 minutes–1 hour 5 minutes, or until the crumb topping is light golden brown and the filling is set. Serve warm or cold, cut into squares and dusted with confectioners' sugar.

Strawberry Cake

1. Preheat the oven to 400°F. Grease a 9 x 13-inch jellyroll pan and line with parchment paper.

2. Put the eggs and sugar into a double boiler or a large heatproof bowl set over a saucepan of simmering water. Using an electric handheld mixer, beat together until the mixture is thick and pale and leaves a trail on the surface when the beaters are lifted. Remove from the heat and beat for an additional 2–3 minutes.

3. Sift in half the flour and fold in gently. Fold in the hot water, then sift in the remaining flour and fold in. Spoon the batter into the prepared pan and gently level the surface with a spatula. Bake in the preheated oven for 9–10 minutes, or until risen, golden brown, and springy to the touch. Let cool in the pan for 10 minutes, then turn out onto a wire rack, peel off the lining paper, and let cool completely.

4. To make the filling, blend the eggs yolks, vanilla or custard powder, and ¼ cup of the milk in a bowl until smooth. Pour the rest of the milk into a saucepan and bring to a boil, then pour the hot milk onto the egg mixture and beat together. Pour the mixture back in to the saucepan, add the sugar, and bring to a boil, beating all the time, until smooth and thick. Transfer the pudding to a bowl, cover the surface with plastic wrap, and let cool completely. Beat the cold pudding until smooth, then fold in the whipped cream and vanilla extract.

5. Return the cold cake to the baking pan and spread the cream custard over the top. Arrange the strawberries, pointed side up, on top. Put the gelatin and water into a small saucepan and let stand for 10 minutes, until the gelatin is soft. Add the sugar and lemon juice and heat gently, stirring, until the gelatin has dissolved. Transfer to a bowl and let cool for 15–20 minutes, or until just beginning to thicken. Brush the glaze all over the strawberries and sprinkle with the chopped pistachios. Let stand in a cool place until the glaze has set, then cut into slices to serve.

Makes 15

Ingredients
butter, for greasing
3 eggs
⅔ cup granulated sugar
1 cup all-purpose flour
1 tablespoon hot water

For the Filling
2 egg yolks
2½ tablespoons instant vanilla
  pudding powder or custard
  powder
1 cup milk
⅓ cup granulated sugar
½ cup heavy cream,
  softly whipped
1 teaspoon vanilla extract

For the Topping & Glaze
1¾ pounds strawberries, hulled
1 sheet of gelatin
⅓ cup water
2 tablespoons granulated sugar
1 teaspoon lemon juice
2 tablespoons pistachio nuts,
  finely chopped

Peach Squares

Makes 12

Ingredients

2 cups all-purpose flour,
   plus extra for dusting
2 teaspoons baking powder
1¾ sticks butter, at room
   temperature, diced, plus
   extra for greasing
¾ cup ground almonds
   (almond meal)
½ cup granulated sugar
1 extra-large egg, lightly beaten

For the Topping

2 eggs
⅓ cup granulated sugar
⅔ cup crème fraiche or Greek
   yogurt
finely grated zest of 1 lemon
¼ cup cornstarch
1 (15-ounce) can peach halves
   in juice, drained
2 tablespoons slivered almonds
confectioners' sugar, for dusting

1. To make the cake, sift the flour and baking powder into a large bowl and add the butter. Using your fingertips, rub the butter into the flour until the mixture resembles coarse bread crumbs. Stir in the ground almonds and sugar. Make a well in the center, add the egg, and mix with a blunt knife to form a soft dough. Knead lightly until just smooth, adding a little extra flour if necessary. Wrap the dough in plastic wrap and chill in the refrigerator for 30 minutes.

2. Preheat the oven to 350°F. Grease a 9 x 13-inch jellyroll pan.

3. Put the dough into the prepared pan and, using clean, lightly floured hands, press the dough in a even layer into the bottom and up the sides of the pan. Bake in the preheated oven for 15 minutes.

4. While the cake is baking, prepare the topping. Put the eggs and granulated sugar into a bowl and beat together until thoroughly combined. Whisk in the crème fraiche, lemon zest, and cornstarch.

5. Remove the partly baked cake from the oven. Cut the peach halves into quarters and arrange on the cake. Carefully spoon the topping mixture over the peaches, then sprinkle with the slivered almonds.

6. Return the cake to the oven and bake for 25–35 minutes, or until the topping is set and light golden brown. Let stand in the pan to cool. Serve warm or cold, cut into squares and dusted with confectioners' sugar.

Orange Sheet Cake

1. Preheat the oven to 375°F. Grease an 8 x 12-inch baking pan and sprinkle with the extra cake crumbs.

2. To make the cake, use an electric mixer to beat the egg yolks with half of the sugar and the orange rind until fluffy. Beat the egg whites until forming firm peaks, gradually beating in the remaining sugar as you beat. Fold the whipped egg white into the egg yolk mixture. Add the cake crumbs with the flour, ground almonds, and melted butter and mix to combine.

3. Spoon the batter into the prepared baking pan and smooth it flat. Bake in the preheated oven for about 40–45 minutes. Let cool in the pan for 5 minutes, then transfer to a wire rack to cool completely.

4. To make the glaze, put the sugar, apricot perserves, orange juice, orange liqueur (if using), and orange zest in a saucepan. Boil it down to about two-thirds of the original volume and brush over the cake. Cut the cake into slices and serve.

Makes 12

Ingredients
2 eggs, separated
⅔ cup granulated sugar
grated rind of 1 orange
¼ cup cake crumbs,
   plus extra for sprinkling
2 tablespoons all-purpose flour
1 cup ground almonds
   (almond meal)
1 tablespoon butter, melted,
   plus extra for greasing

For the glaze
⅓ cup granulated sugar
2½ tablespoons apricot
   preserves
1 cup orange juice
1 tablespoon orange liqueur
   (optional)
pared zest of 1 large orange

Chocolate Oat Bars

Makes 12

Ingredients

1½ sticks butter,
  plus extra for greasing
½ cup firmly packed light
  brown sugar
3 tablespoons light corn syrup
1 tablespoon preserved
  ginger syrup
2 pieces preserved ginger,
  finely chopped
4 cups rolled oats

For the Chocolate Glaze

6 ounces semisweet chocolate,
  broken into pieces
3 tablespoons butter

1. Preheat the oven to 350°F. Grease a shallow 11 x 7-inch baking tin.

2. Put the butter, sugar, corn syrup, and ginger syrup into a large saucepan over low heat and heat gently until melted. Remove from the heat and stir in the ginger and oats.

3. Spoon the batter into the prepared pan and smooth the surface. Bake in the preheated oven for 15–20 minutes, or until pale golden brown. Let cool in the pan.

4. To make the glaze, put the chocolate and butter into a double boiler or a heatproof bowl set over a saucepan of simmering water and heat until melted. Stir until smooth, then spread over the cooled oatmeal bars. Chill in the refrigerator for 1 hour, or until set. Cut into 12 bars.

Chocolate Cheesecake Bars

1. Preheat the oven to 325°F. Grease an 8- x 12-inch baking pan that is at least 2 inches deep.

2. To make the crust, sift together the flour, baking powder, and cocoa powder in a large bowl. Rub in the butter and sugar, then add the egg. Mix to a crumbly crust.

3. Spread three-quarters of the crust in the prepared baking pan, pressing firmly into the bottom and up the sides. Put the remainder of the crust to one side.

4. To make the filling, beat together the butter, sugar, and vanilla extract in a large bowl. Gradually beat in the eggs. Add the cheese, cream, and cornstarch and beat until smooth.

5. Spread the cheesecake mixture onto the crust and smooth flat with a spatula. Break the reserved crust mixture apart with your fingertips and sprinkle over the top of the cheesecake mixture.

6. Bake in the preheated oven for 1¼ hours. Let cool completely before removing carefully from the baking pan. Dust with confectioners' sugar, sprinkle with chopped hazelnuts, and cut into bars before serving.

Makes 12

Ingredients
2 cups all-purpose flour
2 teaspoons baking powder
3 tablespoons unsweetened
  cocoa powder
1¼ sticks butter, cut into small
  dice, plus extra for greasing
¾ cup granulated sugar
1 egg

For the filling
2¼ sticks butter, softened
1⅓ cups granulated sugar
2 teaspoons vanilla extract
4 eggs, lightly beaten
3 cups reduced-fat cream cheese
½ cup heavy cream
1 tablespoon cornstarch
confectioners' sugar and
  chopped hazelnuts, for
  sprinkling

Cheesecakes and Cakes

Blueberry Cheesecake

Serves 10

Ingredients
sunflower oil, for brushing
6 tablespoons butter
1¾ cups finely crushed graham
*   crackers or plain cookies*
1¾ cups cream cheese
2 extra-large eggs
¾ cup granulated sugar
1½ teaspoons vanilla extract
2 cups sour cream

For the Topping
¼ cup granulated sugar
1 cup water
1¾ cups fresh blueberries
1 teaspoon arrowroot powder

1. Preheat the oven to 375°F. Brush an 8-inch round springform cake pan with oil.

2. Melt the butter in a saucepan over low heat. Stir in the crackers, then press into the bottom of the prepared pan.

3. Put the cream cheese, eggs, ½ cup of the sugar, and ½ teaspoon of the vanilla extract in a food processor. Process until smooth. Pour over the crust and smooth the top. Place on a baking sheet and bake in the preheated oven for 20 minutes, or until set. Remove from the oven and let stand for 20 minutes. Leave the oven on.

4. Mix the sour cream with the remaining sugar and vanilla extract in a bowl. Spoon the cream mixture over the cheesecake. Return to the oven for 10 minutes, let cool, then cover with plastic wrap and chill in the refrigerator for 8 hours, or overnight.

5. To make the topping, put the sugar and 2 tablespoons of the water in a saucepan over low heat and stir until the sugar has dissolved. Increase the heat, add the blueberries, cover, and cook for a few minutes, or until they begin to soften. Remove from the heat. Mix the arrowroot powder and remaining water in a bowl, add to the blueberries, and stir until smooth. Return to low heat. Cook until the juice thickens and turns translucent. Let cool. Remove the cheesecake from the pan 1 hour before serving. Spoon over the blueberry topping and chill until ready to serve.

Classic Cheesecake

1. To make the crust, sift the flour into a bowl and, using an electric mixer with a dough hook, beat in the sugar, vanilla extract, and butter. Beat in the egg and knead to a smooth dough. Form into a ball, wrap in plastic wrap, and put into the refrigerator for 1 hour.

2. Preheat the oven to 350°F. Line the bottom of an 11-inch springform cake pan with parchment paper and grease the sides with a little butter.

3. Turn the dough out onto a floured surface and roll out to a thickness of about ¼ inch. Line the bottom and the sides of the pan with the dough and prick the bottom with a fork several times. Bake in the preheated oven for about 15 minutes.

4. To make the topping, put the egg whites and sugar in a bowl and beat until forming peaks. In a separate bowl, beat together the cheese, cornstarch, vanilla seeds, egg yolks, cream, and lemon rind and juice. Fold the beaten egg white into the cheese mixture in two stages. This will help to make the cheesecake nice and light.

5. Spread the topping onto the partly baked crust and smooth flat with a spatula. Return the cheesecake to the oven for about 1 hour. Take the cheesecake out of the oven and let cool in the pan. Then remove from the pan and dust with confectioners' sugar to serve.

Serves 12

Ingredients
1⅔ cups all-purpose flour,
   plus extra for dusting
¼ cup granulated sugar
1 teaspoon vanilla extract
1 stick butter, softened,
   plus extra for greasing
1 egg

For the Topping
5 eggs, separated
1 cup granulated sugar
3½ cups reduced-fat
   cream cheese
½ cup cornstarch
seeds from 1 vanilla bean
1¼ cups heavy cream
grated rind of 1 lemon
2 tablespoons lemon juice
confectioners' sugar, for dusting

Easy Cheesecake

Serves 8

Ingredients

1½ tablespoons butter,
  for greasing
1 cup fresh white bread crumbs
3¼ cups reduced-fat
  cream cheese
½ cup sour cream
3 eggs
¾ cup granulated sugar
¼ cup cornstarch
½ cup sunflower oil
½ cup milk
confectioners' sugar, for dusting

1. Preheat the oven to 325°F. Grease a 9-inch diameter springform cake pan with butter and sprinkle the bread crumbs over the bottom.

2. To make the cheesecake filling, mix together the cheese, sour cream, eggs, sugar, cornstarch, oil, and milk and beat to a smooth, creamy consistency.

3. Spoon the cheesecake batter into the pan, smooth with a spatula, and bake in the preheated oven for 1 hour.

4. Let the cheesecake cool in the pan before removing and carefully placing on a serving plate. Dust with confectioners' sugar to serve.

Caramel Pecan Cheesecake

1. Preheat the oven to 325°F. Lightly grease a 9-inch round springform cake pan.

2. Put the crushed crackers and the nuts into a bowl and stir in the butter. Press into the bottom of the prepared cake pan. Chill in the refrigerator while making the filling.

3. Put the cheese and sugars into a large bowl and beat together until creamy. Gradually beat in the eggs and vanilla extract, then fold in the sour cream and cornstarch. Pour over the cookie crust.

4. Place on a baking sheet and bake in the preheated oven for 45–50 minutes, or until just set (the middle should still wobble slightly). Turn off the heat, open the oven door, and let the cheesecake stand in the oven until cold. Chill in the refrigerator for 3–4 hours or overnight.

5. Unclip the pan and transfer the cheesecake to a serving plate. To make the topping, gently spread the dulce du leche over the top of the cheesecake and sprinkle with the nuts.

Serves 8

Ingredients
2¼ cups finely crushed graham
 crackers or plain cookies
¼ cup finely chopped pecans
6 tablespoons butter, melted,
 plus extra for greasing
2½ cups cream cheese
2 tablespoons packed light
 brown sugar
½ cup granulated sugar
3 extra-large eggs, beaten
1 teaspoon vanilla extract
1¼ cups sour cream
2 tablespoons cornstarch

For the Topping
¼ cup dulce du leche
 (caramel sauce)
¼ cup chopped pecans

Cherry Cheesecake

Serves 10

Ingredients

1 stick butter, melted,
   plus extra for greasing
⅔ cup reduced-fat cream cheese
½ cup milk
½ cup granulated sugar
2 teaspoons vanilla extract
2⅓ cups all-purpose flour,
   plus extra for dusting
2 teaspoons baking powder

For the Filling

4 tablespoons butter, softened
½ cup granulated sugar
1 teaspoon vanilla extract
2 tablespoons lemon juice
2 eggs, separated
2 cups reduced-fat cream cheese
¾ cup all-purpose flour
1 teaspoon baking powder
3 tablespoons cornstarch
2 cups pitted fresh dark
   sweet cherries

For the Topping

¾ cup slivered almonds
⅔ cup all-purpose flour
3 tablespoons butter
¼ cup granulated sugar
confectioners' sugar, for dusting

1. Preheat the oven to 325°F. Line the bottom of a 10½-inch springform cake pan with parchment paper and grease the sides with butter.

2. To make the crust, first mix the melted butter with the cheese, milk, sugar, and vanilla extract in a bowl. Sift together the flour and baking powder and beat into the cheese mixture. Knead the mixture vigorously on a floured surface and press the dough into the bottom and up the sides of the pan. Place in the refrigerator.

3. To make the filling, put the butter and half of the sugar in a large bowl and use an electric mixer to beat until fluffy. Add the vanilla extract and lemon juice and continue beating. Beat the egg yolks into the butter mixture and beat in the cheese. Sift together the flour, baking powder, and cornstarch into another large bowl and then add the cheese mixture gradually, beating continuously.

4. Remove the crust from the refrigerator. Beat the egg whites until stiff, then beat in the remaining sugar until they form peaks. Use a spatula to fold the whipped egg white into the cheese mixture in two stages. Spread half of the filling over the crust in the pan and place half of the cherries on top. Spread the remaining filling over the top and smooth flat. Place the remaining cherries on top.

5. To make the topping, mix the almonds, flour, butter, and sugar in a bowl and rub with your fingers until crumbly. Sprinkle the crumb mixture on top of the cheesecake filling.

6. Bake in the preheated oven for about 40 minutes, covering with aluminum foil toward the end of the cooking time. Let the cooked cheesecake rest in the pan for about 30 minutes. Dust with confectioners' sugar and serve.

Apple & Raisin Cheesecake

1. Start by preparing the raisins for the topping. Put the raisins into a small bowl, pour the black tea over them, and let soak for an hour.

2. To make the crust, sift together the flour and baking powder into a bowl and stir in the sugar. Add the diced butter and rub into the flour mixture between your fingers until the mixture is loose and crumbly. Add the egg, vanilla extract, and rum and knead vigorously to make a firm dough. Wrap in plastic wrap and let rest in the refrigerator for 30 minutes.

3. Preheat the oven to 325°F. Grease and line the bottom of an 11-inch diameter springform cake pan and grease the sides.

4. Roll out the dough on a floured surface to the diameter of the pan, place the dough in the greased pan, and prick with a fork several times. Bake in the preheated oven for about 20 minutes, until lightly browned. Leave the oven on.

5. To make the filling, put the cheese, lemon juice, and cornstarch in a large bowl and beat together until smooth and creamy. In a separate bowl, beat the eggs, sugar, and vanilla extract until fluffy. Stir the egg mixture into the cheese mixture.

6. To make the topping, pour the soaked raisins into a strainer and let drain. Peel, quarter, and core the apples. Use a knife to cut 4–5 crosses ¼ inch deep in the outer side of each quarter.

7. Spoon the cheese mixture over the crust in the pan and smooth flat with a spatula. Arrange the apple quarters on the cake and sprinkle the raisins on top. Return the cheesecake to the oven and bake for an additional 50 minutes, then let cool and dust with confectioners' sugar to serve.

Serves 12

Ingredients
2 cups all-purpose flour,
  plus extra for dusting
large pinch of baking powder
⅓ cup granulated sugar
1¼ sticks butter, cut into small
  dice, plus extra for greasing
1 egg, lightly beaten
1 teaspoon vanilla extract
4 teaspoons rum

For the Filling
3¼ cups reduced-fat
  cream cheese
2 tablespoons lemon juice
¼ cup cornstarch
3 eggs
½ cup granulated sugar
1 teaspoon vanilla extract

For the Topping
¼ cup raisins
½ cup regular black tea
4 Pippin apples
confectioners' sugar, for dusting

Lemon Cheesecake

Serves 6

Ingredients

4 tablespoons butter,
  plus extra for greasing
1½ cups crushed gingersnaps
3 lemons
1¼ cups ricotta cheese
1 cup Greek-style yogurt
4 eggs, beaten
1 tablespoon cornstarch
½ cup granulated sugar
strips of lemon zest, to decorate
confectioners' sugar, for dusting

1. Preheat the oven to 350°F. Grease an 8-inch round springform cake pan and line with parchment paper.

2. Melt the butter in a saucepan and stir in the cookie crumbs. Press into the bottom of the prepared cake pan. Chill until firm.

3. Meanwhile, finely grate the rind from the lemons into a bowl and squeeze the juice. Add the ricotta, yogurt, eggs, cornstarch, and granulated sugar and beat until a smooth batter is formed.

4. Carefully spoon the batter into the prepared pan. Bake in the preheated oven for 40–45 minutes, or until just firm and golden brown.

5. Cool the cheesecake completely in the pan, then run a knife around the edge to loosen and turn out onto a serving plate. Decorate with lemon zest and dust with confectioners' sugar.

Mixed Berry Meringue Cake

1. Preheat the oven to 350°F. Grease an 11-inch diameter springform cake pan and lightly dust with flour. Put the egg whites in a bowl in the refrigerator to use later in the meringue.

2. To make the crust, use an electric mixer to beat the egg yolks, sugar, and vanilla extract in a bowl, until fluffy.

3. Bring the milk and butter to a boil in a small pan over medium heat, pour into the egg-and-sugar mixture, and beat together thoroughly until thick. Sift the flour and baking powder into the bowl and fold in gently.

4. Pour the cake batter into the pan and bake in the preheated oven for about 18 minutes, until pale golden brown. Remove from the oven and let cool for a short time. Leave the oven on.

5. To make the meringue, using a handheld electric mixer, beat the egg whites until holding stiff peaks. Gradually beat in the sugar, one tablespoon at a time until the mixture is firm and glossy. Fold in the cornstarch. Pick through the berries, reserving 1 tablespoon of each kind, then gently fold the remaining berries into the meringue. Spread the fruity meringue mixture over the baked cake crust.

6. Sprinkle the reserved berries on top of the meringue. Turn the oven up to 425°F, place the cake on the middle shelf, and bake for 10–15 minutes. Dust with confectioners' sugar when cool and then serve.

Serves 12

Ingredients
3 egg yolks
¾ cup granulated sugar
2 teaspoons vanilla extract
½ cup milk
1 stick butter, plus extra
* for greasing*
2¼ cups all-purpose flour,
* plus extra for dusting*
2 teaspoons baking powder

For the Meringue
3 egg whites
½ cup superfine sugar or
* granulated sugar*
1 teaspoon cornstarch
1⅓ cups blueberries
1⅓ cups red currants, stems
* removed, or other berries*
* of your choice, halved or*
* quartered if large*
confectioners' sugar, for dusting

Plum Cheesecake

Serves 10

Ingredients

2 cups all-purpose flour, plus
    extra for dusting
½ teaspoon baking powder
1 stick butter, cut into small
    dice, plus extra for greasing
1 egg
½ cup granulated sugar
¼ teaspoon ground cinnamon

For the Filling

3 eggs
¾ cup granulated sugar
1 teaspoon vanilla extract
juice of ½ lemon
3¼ cups reduced-fat
    cream cheese
3 tablespoons cornstarch

For the Topping

9 plums (about 1¼ pounds)
2 tablespoons packed light
    brown sugar

1. To make the crust, sift together the flour and baking powder in a bowl. Add the other ingredients and use your hands to knead the mixture to a smooth dough. Wrap the dough in plastic wrap and let rest in the refrigerator for 30 minutes.

2. To make the filling, put the eggs, sugar, and vanilla extract in a bowl and beat with an electric mixer until fluffy. Add the lemon juice, cheese, and cornstarch and mix until smooth and creamy.

3. Preheat the oven to 400°F. Grease a 10½-inch diameter springform cake pan and lightly dust with flour.

4. Remove the dough from the refrigerator, knead and roll on a lightly floured surface until it is ¼ inch thick and slightly larger than the pan. Line the prepared pan with the dough, pressing up the sides, and prick the bottom with a fork several times. Spread the filling over the bottom and smooth using a spatula. Bake in the preheated oven for about 30 minutes. Meanwhile, wash the plums, remove the pits, and cut them into quarters.

5. Remove the cheesecake from the oven, leaving the oven on. Arrange the plums on top and sprinkle with the brown sugar. Return the cheesecake to the oven and bake for an additional 40 minutes. Let cool then serve.

Mocha Cheesecake

1. Grease an 8-inch round springform cake pan. Melt the butter in a large saucepan. Remove from the heat. Add the crushed cookies and mix well. Spoon over the bottom of the prepared pan and press down evenly. Chill until firm.

2. Put the chocolate and coffee liquid into a heatproof bowl set over a saucepan of gently simmering water until melted. Cool slightly. Pour the cold water into a separate heatproof bowl, sprinkle the gelatin evenly over the surface, and let stand for 5 minutes, until spongy. Set the bowl over a saucepan of gently simmering water until melted. Remove from the heat. (Alternatively, use a double boiler.)

3. Put the ricotta cheese, sugar, and chocolate mixture into a large bowl and beat together with an electric handheld mixer until smooth, then beat in the melted gelatin. Fold in the cream, then spoon over the cookie crust. Chill for at least 3 hours or until firm.

4. Dredge the top of the cheesecake with sifted cocoa powder, remove from the pan, and transfer to a serving plate. Serve with whipped cream.

Serves 6

Ingredients
6 tablespoons butter, plus extra
  for greasing
1¾ cups crushed chocolate
  cookies

For the Filling
6 ounces semisweet chocolate,
  broken into pieces
1 tablespoon instant espresso
  powder dissolved in
  ⅓ cup boiling water
⅓ cup cold water
2 tablespoons powdered gelatin
1⅔ cups ricotta cheese
⅓ cup granulated sugar
1 cup heavy cream, gently
  whipped
unsweetened cocoa powder,
  to decorate
whipped cream, to serve

Apricot Cream Cake

Serves 12

Ingredients

2 cups all-purpose flour
1 teaspoon baking powder
⅓ cup granulated sugar
1 teaspoon vanilla extract
1 egg
1 stick butter, plus extra
    for greasing

For the Filling

3 egg whites
1 cup heavy cream
1¼ cups sour cream
1¼ cups reduced-fat cream
    cheese
¾ cup granulated sugar
3 egg yolks
1 tablespoon lemon juice
3 tablespoons cornstarch

For the Apricot Layer

11 apricots (about 1 pound)
confectioners' sugar, for dusting

1. To make the crust, sift together the flour and baking powder in a bowl. Add the other ingredients and use your hands to knead the mixture to a smooth dough. Wrap the dough in plastic wrap and let rest in the refrigerator for 30 minutes.

2. Preheat the oven to 350°F. Grease an 11-inch springform cake pan. Line the bottom of the prepared pan with half of the dough. Shape the remaining dough into a long roll and press around the edge of the dough circle and against the side of the pan to create a 1¼-inch raised rim. Bake the dough shell in the preheated oven for about 12 minutes, remove from the oven, and let cool for 5 minutes. Lower the oven temperature to 325°F.

3. To make the filling, put the egg whites in a bowl and, using a handheld electric mixer on its fastest setting, beat until it makes stiff peaks. In another bowl, whip the heavy cream until forming firm peaks. Put the sour cream, cheese, sugar, egg yolks, lemon juice, and cornstarch in a large bowl and beat together until smooth and creamy. Fold in the heavy cream and the egg whites carefully.

4. To make the apricot layer, rinse the apricots, cut in half, and remove the pits. Arrange the fruit on the crust. Cover with the cheese mixture and smooth using a spatula.

5. Return the cheesecake to the oven and bake for an additional 55 minutes at the lower temperature. Cover with aluminum foil after about 40 minutes to prevent the surface from getting too brown. Turn the oven off. Let the baked cheesecake stand in the oven with the door slightly open for about 15 minutes, then remove from the oven and let cool in the pan. Dust with confectioners' sugar and serve.

Gooseberry Cream Cake

1. Sift the flour into a bowl and stir in the yeast and sugar. Add the butter and rub into the flour with your fingertips to make fine bread crumbs. Make a well in the center and pour in the lukewarm milk. Mix with a blunt knife to a soft dough.

2. Knead on a lightly floured surface for 5–6 minutes, until smooth and elastic. Place the dough in a bowl, cover, and let stand in a warm place for about 1 hour, or until the dough has doubled in size.

3. Preheat the oven to 350°F. Grease a 9-inch round springform pan.

4. Turn out the dough onto a floured surface and knead for 1–2 minutes. Roll out to a 10-inch circle and place in the prepared pan, gently easing the dough up the sides of the pan.

5. To make the filling, put the cream cheese, sugar, and vanilla extract in a bowl and beat together until smooth. Gradually beat in the eggs, then stir in the sour cream and orange zest.

6. Spoon the batter into the pan, then spread the gooseberries over the top. Place the pan on a baking sheet and bake in the preheated oven for 30 minutes.

7. To make the topping, put the egg and sugar into a bowl and, using a handheld electric mixer, beat together until pale and thick. Beat in the melted butter, then sift the flour over the top and gently fold in.

8. Remove the cake from the oven and gently spoon the topping over the partly set filling. Return to the oven and bake for an additional 25–30 minutes, or until the topping is set and golden brown. Let cool in the pan.

Serves 8

Ingredients
1¼ cups white bread flour,
 plus extra for dusting
1 teaspoon active dry yeast
2 tablespoons granulated sugar
2 tablespoons butter, softened,
 plus extra for greasing
½ cup lukewarm milk

For the Filling
1 cup reduced-fat cream cheese
¼ cup granulated sugar
1 teaspoon vanilla extract
2 eggs, lightly beaten
1¼ cups sour cream
grated zest of ½ orange
2 cups trimmed fresh
 gooseberries or 1⅓ cups
 canned gooseberries

For the Topping
1 egg, lightly beaten
¼ cup granulated sugar
3 tablespoons unsalted butter,
 melted
2 tablespoons all-purpose flour

Apple Caramel Upside-Down Cake

Serves 6

Ingredients

oil or melted butter,
for greasing
1⅓ cups all-purpose flour
1 tablespoon baking powder
1½ sticks unsalted butter,
softened
¾ cup granulated sugar
3 eggs, beaten
1 teaspoon vanilla extract
finely grated rind of 1 lemon

For the Toffee Apple Topping

4 tablespoons unsalted butter
½ cup granulated sugar
1 tablespoon water
4 Pippin or other sweet
crisp apples
2 tablespoons lemon juice

1. Preheat the oven to 350°F. Grease a 9-inch round cake pan with a solid bottom.

2. For the toffee apple topping, put the butter and sugar into a heavy saucepan with the water and heat gently until melted, then bring to a boil. Reduce the heat and cook, stirring, until it turns to a deep golden caramel color. Pour quickly into the prepared pan, tilting to cover the bottom evenly.

3. Peel, core, and thickly slice the apples, toss with the lemon juice, and spread evenly over the bottom of the pan.

4. Sift the flour and baking powder into a large bowl and add the butter, sugar, eggs, and vanilla extract. Beat well until the batter is smooth, then stir in the lemon rind.

5. Spoon the batter over the apples and smooth the surface with a spatula. Bake in the preheated oven for 40–50 minutes, or until risen and golden brown.

6. Let cool in the pan for 2–3 minutes, then turn out carefully onto a warmed serving plate.

Iced Pound Cake

1. Preheat the oven to 325°F. Grease a 9-inch loaf pan and line with parchment paper.

2. Put the butter and granulated sugar in a large bowl and beat together until pale and creamy. Beat in the lemon rind, then gradually beat in the eggs. Sift the all-purpose flour and baking powder into the mixture and fold in gently until thoroughly incorporated. Fold in the milk and lemon juice.

3. Spoon the batter into the prepared pan and bake in the preheated oven for 1–1¼ hours, or until well risen, golden brown, and a toothpick inserted into the center comes out clean. Cool in the pan for 15 minutes, then turn out onto a wire rack to cool completely.

4. For the icing, sift the confectioners' sugar into a bowl. Add the lemon juice and stir to make a smooth and thick icing. Gently spread the icing over the top of the cake. Drizzle the warmed lemon curd over the icing and drag a toothpick through the icing to create a swirled effect.

Serves 10

Ingredients

1½ sticks unsalted butter, softened, plus extra for greasing
¾ cup granulated sugar
finely grated rind of 1 lemon
3 eggs, lightly beaten
2¼ cups all-purpose flour
1 teaspoon baking powder
2 tablespoons milk
1 tablespoon lemon juice

For the Icing

1⅓ cups confectioners' sugar
2–3 tablespoons lemon juice
2 teaspoons lemon curd, warmed

Red Velvet Cake

1. Preheat the oven to 375°F. Grease two 9-inch cake pans and line with parchment paper.

2. Put the butter, water, and cocoa powder into a small saucepan and heat gently, without boiling, stirring until melted and smooth. Remove from the heat and let cool slightly.

3. Beat together the eggs, buttermilk, vanilla extract, and food coloring in a bowl until frothy. Beat in the butter mixture. Sift together the flour, cornstarch, and baking powder, then stir quickly and evenly into the batter with the granulated sugar.

4. Divide the batter between the prepared pans and bake in the preheated oven for 25–30 minutes, or until risen and firm to the touch. Let cool in the pans for 3–4 minutes, then turn out onto a wire rack to cool completely.

5. To make the frosting, beat together all the ingredients until smooth. Use about half of the frosting to sandwich the cakes together, then spread the remainder over the top, swirling with a spatula.

Serves 12

Ingredients
2 sticks unsalted butter, plus extra for greasing
¼ cup water
⅔ cup unsweetened cocoa powder
3 eggs, beaten
1 cup buttermilk
2 teaspoons vanilla extract
2 tablespoons red edible food coloring
2¼ cups all-purpose flour
⅓ cup cornstarch
1½ teaspoons baking powder
1⅓ cups granulated sugar

For the Frosting
1 cup cream cheese
3 tablespoons unsalted butter
3 tablespoons granulated sugar
1 teaspoon vanilla extract

Marble Cake

Serves 8

Ingredients:

2 ounces semisweet chocolate,
  broken into pieces
3 tablespoons milk
5 tablespoons unsalted butter,
  plus extra for greasing
⅓ cup granulated sugar
1 egg, beaten
3 tablespoons sour cream
1 cup all-purpose flour,
  plus extra for dusting
1½ teaspoons baking powder
½ teaspoon vanilla extract

1. Preheat the oven to 325°F. Grease an 8½-inch loaf pan and line the bottom with nonstick parchment paper. Dust a little flour around the inside of the pan, shaking out the excess.

2. Put the chocolate and milk into a double boiler or a small heatproof bowl set over a saucepan of simmering water. Heat gently until just melted. Remove from the heat.

3. Cream together the butter and sugar until light and fluffy. Beat in the egg and sour cream. Sift the flour and baking powder over the mixture, then fold in lightly and evenly using a metal spoon.

4. Spoon half the batter into a separate bowl and stir in the chocolate mixture. Add the vanilla extract to the plain mixture. Spoon the chocolate and vanilla batters alternately into the prepared loaf pan, swirling lightly with a knife or toothpick to create a marbled effect. Bake in the preheated oven for 40–45 minutes, or until well-risen and firm to the touch.

5. Cool in the pan for 10 minutes, then turn out and finish cooling on a wire rack.

Classic Chocolate Cake

1. Preheat the oven to 350°F. Grease two 8-inch cake pans and line with parchment paper.

2. Blend the cocoa powder and water to a smooth paste and set aside. Put the butter, granulated sugar, and brown sugar into a large bowl and beat together until pale and creamy. Gradually beat in the eggs, then stir in the cocoa paste and vanilla extract.

3. Sift in the flour and baking powder and fold in gently. Divide the batter between the prepared pans. Bake in the preheated oven for 25–30 minutes, or until risen and just springy to the touch. Let cool in the pans for 5 minutes, then turn out onto a wire rack to cool completely.

4. To make the frosting, put the chocolate and butter into a double boiler or a heatproof bowl set over a saucepan of simmering water and heat until melted. Remove from the heat and stir in the cream. Let cool for 20 minutes, then chill in the refrigerator for 40–50 minutes, stirring occasionally, until thick enough to spread.

5. Sandwich the cakes together with one-third of the frosting, then spread the remainder over the top and sides of the cake.

Serves 10

Ingredients
⅔ cup unsweetened cocoa
  powder
½ cup boiling water
1¾ sticks butter, softened,
  plus extra for greasing
⅔ cup granulated sugar
⅓ cup firmly packed light
  brown sugar
4 eggs, beaten
1 teaspoon vanilla extract
1⅔ cups all-purpose flour
1½ teaspoons baking powder

For the Frosting
8 ounces semisweet chocolate,
  broken into pieces
1 stick unsalted butter
½ cup heavy cream

Coffee Bundt Cake

Serves 14

Ingredients
3¼ cups all-purpose flour,
    plus extra for dusting
1 tablespoon baking powder
1 teaspoon baking soda
3 tablespoons espresso coffee
    powder
2¼ sticks salted butter,
    softened, plus extra
    for greasing
½ cup firmly packed light
    brown sugar
1 cup maple syrup
3 eggs, beaten
1 cup buttermilk
1 cup heavy cream

For the Decoration
¼ cup maple syrup
1⅔ cups confectioners' sugar
1 tablespoon unsalted butter,
    melted
20 chocolate-coated coffee
    beans

1. Preheat the oven to 350°F. Grease and lightly flour a 3-quart Bundt pan.

2. Sift the flour, baking powder, baking soda, and coffee powder into a bowl. In a separate bowl, beat together the butter and brown sugar until pale and creamy. Gradually beat in the maple syrup. Beat in the eggs slowly, adding 3 tablespoons of the flour mixture to prevent it from curdling.

3. Mix together the buttermilk and cream and add half to the butter mixture. Sprinkle in half of the flour mixture and fold gently together. Add the remaining buttermilk and flour mixtures and mix together gently until just combined.

4. Spoon the batter into the prepared pan and smooth the surface. Bake in the preheated oven for about 50 minutes, or until well risen and a toothpick inserted into the center comes out clean. Let cool in the pan for 10 minutes, then loosen with a knife and turn out onto a wire rack to cool completely.

5. To decorate, beat the maple syrup in a bowl with 1¼ cups of the confectioners' sugar and the butter until smooth and thickly coating the back of a wooden spoon. Transfer the cake to a serving plate and spoon the icing around the top of the cake so it starts to run down the sides.

6. Beat the remaining confectioners' sugar in a small bowl with 1½–2 teaspoons of water to make a smooth paste. Using a teaspoon, drizzle the icing over the cake. Sprinkle the coffee beans over the top.

Maple & Pecan Bundt Cake

1. Preheat the oven to 325°F. Grease and lightly flour a 2-quart Bundt pan.

2. Put the butter and brown sugar into a bowl and beat together until pale and fluffy. Gradually beat in the eggs, then stir in the nuts, maple syrup, and sour cream. Sift in the flour and baking powder and fold in thoroughly.

3. Spoon the batter into the prepared pan and gently smooth the surface. Bake in the preheated oven for 45–50 minutes, or until the cake is firm and golden brown and a toothpick inserted into the center comes out clean. Let cool in the pan for 10 minutes, then turn out onto a wire rack to cool completely.

4. To make the icing, mix the confectioners' sugar, maple syrup, and enough water to make a smooth icing. Spoon the icing over the top of the cake, letting it run down the sides. Decorate with the chopped nuts and let set.

Serves 10

Ingredients

1¾ sticks butter, softened,
  plus extra for greasing
1 cup firmly packed light brown
  sugar
3 extra-large eggs, beaten
½ cup finely chopped pecans,
  plus extra to decorate
¼ cup maple syrup
⅔ cup sour cream
1¾ cups all-purpose flour, plus
  extra for dusting
2¾ teaspoons baking powder

For the Icing

⅔ cup confectioners' sugar,
  sifted
1 tablespoon maple syrup
1–2 tablespoons lukewarm
water

Lemon Drizzle Loaf

Serves 8–10

Ingredients

oil or melted butter,
  for greasing
1⅓ cups all-purpose flour
1 tablespoon baking powder
1½ sticks unsalted butter,
  softened
¾ cup granulated sugar
3 eggs, beaten
1 egg yolk
finely grated rind of 1 lemon
2 tablespoons lemon juice
fine strips of lemon zest,
  to decorate

For the Syrup

⅔ cup confectioners' sugar
3 tablespoons lemon juice

1. Preheat the oven to 350°F. Grease and line an 8-inch loaf pan.

2. Sift the flour and baking powder into a large bowl and add the butter, granulated sugar, eggs, and egg yolk. Beat well until the batter is smooth, then stir in the lemon rind and juice.

3. Spoon the batter into the prepared pan and smooth the surface with a spatula. Bake in the preheated oven for 40–50 minutes, or until well risen, firm, and golden brown.

4. Remove the pan from the oven and transfer to a wire rack. For the syrup, put the confectioners' sugar and lemon juice into a saucepan and heat gently without boiling, stirring until the sugar dissolves.

5. Prick the top of the loaf several times with a toothpick and spoon the syrup over it. Let cool completely in the pan, then turn out, sprinkle with strips of lemon zest, and cut into slices.

How to make the perfect cup of tea:

Heat plenty of freshly drawn water until just before it reaches a boil, swirl some of this hot water in your teapot, then discard. Add one heaping teaspoon of tea leaves per person plus one for the pot. Pour the hot water over the tea leaves in the pot and let stand for 3–6 minutes, depending on the size of tea leaf. Give the pot a good stir before pouring through a strainer into cups. Add cold, fresh milk or lemon juice to taste.

Ice Box Chocolate Cake

1. Grease and line an 8½-inch loaf pan. Put the chocolate, butter, coffee, sugar, and vanilla extract into a saucepan over low heat and stir until the chocolate and butter have melted, the sugar has dissolved, and the mixture is well combined.

2. Stir in the crushed cookies, raisins, and walnuts and stir well.

3. Spoon the batter into the prepared loaf pan. Let set in the refrigerator for 1–2 hours, then turn out and cut into thin slices to serve.

Serves 6–8

Ingredients
8 ounces semisweet chocolate
2 sticks unsalted butter,
  plus extra for greasing
3 tablespoons black coffee
¼ cup firmly packed light
  brown sugar
a few drops of vanilla extract
2 cups crushed graham
  crackers or plain cookies
½ cup raisins
⅔ cup chopped walnuts

Carrot Cake

Serves 10

Ingredients

*oil or melted butter,
  for greasing*
1⅓ cups all-purpose flour
1 tablespoon baking powder
1 teaspoon ground cinnamon
½ teaspoon ground ginger
*1½ sticks unsalted butter,
  softened*
*¾ cup firmly packed light
  brown sugar*
3 eggs, beaten
2 tablespoons orange juice
2 cups shredded carrots
*½ cup chopped pecans,
  plus extra pecan halves
  to decorate*

For the Frosting

¼ cup cream cheese
2 cups confectioners' sugar
finely grated rind of 1 orange
*1 tablespoon orange juice,
  plus extra if needed*

1. Preheat the oven to 325°F. Grease and line a deep 9-inch round cake pan.

2. Sift the flour, baking powder, cinnamon, and ginger into a bowl and add the butter, brown sugar, and eggs. Beat well until smooth, then stir in the orange juice, carrots, and chopped pecans.

3. Spoon the batter into the prepared pan and smooth the top. Bake in the preheated oven for 1 hour–1 hour 10 minutes, or until risen, firm, and golden brown.

4. Let cool in the pan for 10 minutes, then turn out onto a wire rack to cool completely.

5. For the frosting, place all the ingredients in a bowl and beat until smooth and thick, adding more orange juice, if necessary. Spread over the top of the cake and decorate with pecan halves.

Country Fruitcake

1. Preheat the oven to 325°F. Grease and line a deep 8-inch round cake pan.

2. Sift the flours, baking powder, and nutmeg into a large bowl, adding any bran left in the sifter. Add the butter, brown sugar, eggs, and vanilla extract. Beat well until the batter is smooth, then stir in the milk and mixed dried fruit.

3. Spoon the batter into the prepared pan and smooth with a spatula. Sprinkle the raw brown sugar evenly over the surface. Bake in the preheated oven for 1 hour 20 minutes–1 hour 30 minutes, or until risen, firm, and golden brown.

4. Let cool in the pan for about 20 minutes, then turn out onto a wire rack to cool completely.

Serves 10

Ingredients:

*oil or melted butter,
  for greasing
1⅓ cups all-purpose white flour
⅔ cup whole-wheat flour
2 teaspoons baking powder
½ teaspoon ground nutmeg
1½ sticks unsalted butter,
  softened
¾ cup firmly packed light
  brown sugar
3 eggs, beaten
1 teaspoon vanilla extract
1 tablespoon milk
1 cup mixed dried fruit
1 tablespoon raw brown sugar*

Boston Cream Pie

Serves 10

Ingredients

4 extra-large eggs, beaten
⅔ cup granulated sugar
1 cup all-purpose flour
3 tablespoons butter, melted
and cooled, plus extra for
greasing

For the Pastry Cream

2 eggs
¼ cup granulated sugar
1 teaspoon vanilla extract
2 tablespoons all-purpose flour
2 tablespoons cornstarch
1¼ cups milk
⅔ cup heavy cream,
gently whipped

For the Chocolate Glaze

4 ounces semisweet chocolate,
grated
1 tablespoon light corn syrup
2 tablespoons unsalted butter
⅔ cup heavy cream

1. Preheat the oven to 350°F. Grease two 9-inch can pans and line with parchment paper.

2. Put the eggs and sugar into a double boiler or a heatproof bowl set over a saucepan of simmering water. Using an electric handheld mixer, beat together until the mixture is thick and pale and leaves a trail when the beaters are lifted.

3. Sift in the flour and fold in gently. Pour the butter in a thin stream over the mixture and fold in until just incorporated. Divide the batter between the prepared pans and bake in the preheated oven for 20–25 minutes, or until light golden brown and springy to the touch. Cool in the pans for 5 minutes, then turn out onto a wire rack to cool completely.

4. For the pastry cream, beat together the eggs, sugar, and vanilla extract. Blend the flour and cornstarch to a paste with ¼ cup of the milk, then beat into the egg mixture. Heat the remaining milk until almost boiling and pour onto the egg mixture, stirring all the time. Return to the saucepan and cook over low heat, beating all the time, until smooth and thickened. Pour into a bowl and cover with dampened wax paper. Let stand until cold, then fold in the whipped cream.

5. For the glaze, put the chocolate, corn syrup, and butter into a heatproof bowl. Heat the cream until almost boiling then pour it over the chocolate. Let stand for 1 minute, then stir until smooth.

6. To assemble, sandwich the sponges together with the pastry cream. Spread the chocolate glaze over the top of the cake.

Dessert
Cakes

Meringue Torte

Serves 12

Ingredients

2⅓ cups all-purpose flour,
    plus extra for dusting
2 teaspoons baking powder
¾ cup granulated sugar
1¼ sticks butter, room
    temperature, plus extra
    for greasing
2 eggs, lightly beaten

For the Topping

3 egg yolks
1 egg
½ cup granulated sugar
1 tablespoon lemon juice
1¼ cups milk
2 cups reduced-fat cream cheese
1¼ sticks butter, melted
⅓ cup instant vanilla pudding
    powder or custard powder

For the Meringue

3 egg whites
¼ cup superfine sugar or
    granulated sugar
2 cups red currants or
    blueberries, sprigs removed
confectioners' sugar, for dusting

1. Preheat the oven to 325°F. Grease an 11-inch cake pan, preferably springform, and line the bottom with parchment paper.

2. To make the crust, sift the flour and baking powder into a bowl and add the sugar, butter, and eggs. Mix together using an electric mixer with a dough hook attachment, then briefly knead with your hands into a smooth dough. Wrap in plastic wrap and let rest in the refrigerator for 30 minutes.

3. Use floured hands to press and smooth the dough evenly into the bottom of the pan.

4. To make the topping, mix together the egg yolks, egg, sugar, and lemon juice in a bowl. Gradually stir in the milk, cheese, melted butter, and vanilla powder or custard powder until the mixture is smooth and has no lumps.

5. Pour the topping mixture over the torte crust and smooth the surface. Bake in the preheated oven for about 30 minutes. Remove the cake, but leave the oven on.

6. To make the meringue, beat the egg whites until almost stiff. Gradually beat in the sugar. Continue beating until the sugar is completely dissolved and the meringue holds stiff peaks.

7. Spread the meringue over the topping. Sprinkle the red currants or blueberries over the top. Return the torte to the oven to bake for about 15 minutes. Let cool before removing from the pan. Dust with confectioners' sugar before slicing and serving.

Raspberry & Cream Cake

1. Preheat the oven to 350°F. Grease an 11-inch springform cake pan.

2. To make the cake, using an electric mixer, beat together the eggs and sugar in a double boiler or a bowl sitting over a saucepan of simmering water until thick and the mixture leaves a trail when the beaters are lifted. Sift together the flour, cornstarch, and baking powder over the beaten egg mixture. Fold in gently.

3. Put the batter into the bottom of the prepared pan and smooth using a spatula. Bake in the preheated oven for 20 minutes, or until springy to the touch.

4. Let the cake cool, then remove from the pan and cut in half horizontally using a long knife. Put the springform ring back around the lower cake half and carefully set the other cake half aside.

5. To make the filling, soak the gelatin in a shallow bowl of cold water for 5 minutes, until softened. Put the cheese, sugar, orange rind, and orange juice into a bowl and beat until smooth and creamy. Remove the gelatin from the water, squeezing out the excess liquid. Place the soft gelatin sheets in a small saucepan and heat gently, stirring until completely dissolved. Remove from the heat and stir into the cheese mixture. Let cool.

6. Whip the heavy cream until it holds firm peaks. When the cheese mixture is almost set, carefully fold in the cream using a spatula. Spoon the raspberries over the cake in the pan. Then spoon the cheese mixture into the pan and spread the raspberries over it. Place the second cake half on top, with the cut side uppermost, and gently press down. Chill the cake in the refrigerator for 3–4 hours.

7. To make the topping, whip the cream with the confectioners' sugar until forming soft peaks. Remove the springform ring. Spread the cream over the cake. Arrange the raspberries on top. Decorate with the grated chocolate and mint leaves and serve.

Serves 12

Ingredients
butter, for greasing
2 eggs
⅓ cup granulated sugar
⅔ cup all-purpose flour
⅔ cup cornstarch
1 teaspoon baking powder

For the Filling
6 sheets of gelatin
*3¼ cups reduced-fat cream
  cheese*
¾ cup granulated sugar
*grated rind and juice of
  1 orange*
2 cups heavy cream
2 cups fresh raspberries

For the Topping
1 cup heavy cream
*2 tablespoons confectioners'
  sugar*
½ cup fresh raspberries
*coarsely grated chocolate
  and fresh mint leaves,
  for decorating*

Strawberry Dessert Cake

Serves 8

Ingredients
2 extra-large eggs
¼ cup granulated sugar
½ cup all-purpose flour
2 tablespoons butter, melted
  and cooled, plus extra
  for greasing

For the Filling
4 sheets of gelatin
finely grated zest and juice
  from 1 lemon
1 cup reduced-fat cream cheese
⅔ cup granulated sugar
1¼ cups heavy cream,
  gently whipped

For the Topping
⅓ cup water
1 sheet of gelatin
2 tablespoons granulated sugar
1 tsp lemon juice
1½ cups hulled and sliced
  strawberries
3–4 tablespoons slivered
  almonds, toasted

1. Preheat the oven to 350°F. Grease a 9-inch round springform pan and line the bottom with parchment paper. Put the eggs and sugar into a double boiler or a heatproof bowl set over a saucepan of simmering water. Using an electric handheld mixer, beat together until the mixture is thick. Remove the bowl from the heat and beat for an additional 2–3 minutes. Sift the flour over the mixture and fold in gently. Pour the melted butter over the top and fold in. Spoon the batter into the prepared pan and level the surface.

2. Bake in the preheated oven for 18–20 minutes, or until risen, golden brown, and springy to the touch. Let cool in the pan for 10 minutes, then turn out onto a wire rack, peel off the lining paper and let cool completely. Lightly grease an 8-inch round springform pan. Using the bottom of the pan as a guide, trim around the edges of the cake so it fits snugly into the bottom of the smaller pan.

3. To make the filling, place the gelatin sheets into a bowl and cover with cold water. Let soak for 5 minutes, until soft. Remove the sheets from the water and squeeze out the excess liquid. Put them into a small saucepan with the lemon juice. Heat gently until the gelatin has completely dissolved. Let cool for 10 minutes. Put the cream cheese, sugar, and lemon zest in a bowl and beat together smooth. Gradually beat in the gelatin mixture, then fold in the whipped cream. Spoon over the cake crust, leveling the surface with a spatula. Chill in the refrigerator for 1 hour.

4. To make the topping, place the water and gelatin in a saucepan and let stand for 10 minutes, until the gelatin is soft. Add the sugar and lemon juice and heat gently, stirring, until the gelatin dissolves. Transfer to a bowl and let cool for 15–20 minutes, or until just beginning to thicken. Arrange the sliced strawberries on top of the cream filling, then spoon the gelatin glaze over them. Chill in the refrigerator for 30 minutes, until the glaze has set. Run a spatula around the edge of the cake, then unclip the pan and transfer to a serving plate. Gently press the slivered almonds around the sides.

Cherry Cake

1. Preheat the oven to 325°F. Grease an 11-inch round cake pan, preferably springform.

2. To make the cake, sift together the flour, baking powder, and cinnamon in a bowl. Add the sugar and diced butter and rub into the flour mixture between your fingers until the mixture resembles coarse bread crumbs. Add the beaten egg and knead the mixture to a smooth dough. Wrap the mixture in plastic wrap and let rest in the refrigerator for 30 minutes.

3. Roll the dough out on a floured surface, put it in the bottom of the prepared pan, press up the sides, and prick several times with a fork. Bake in the preheated oven for about 20 minutes, or until lightly browned, and let stand in the pan to cool. Leave the oven on.

4. To make the filling, mix together the cheese, lemon juice, and cornstarch in a bowl until smooth and creamy. Beat the eggs, sugar, and vanilla extract until light and fluffy and stir into the cheese mixture.

5. Spoon the filling into the cake crust. Arrange the drained cherries over the filling and continue baking for an additional 50 minutes, until set and golden brown. Let cool. Dust with confectioners' sugar before serving.

Serves 12

Ingredients
2 cups all-purpose flour,
  plus extra for dusting
2 teaspoons baking powder
large pinch of cinnamon
½ cup granulated sugar
1 stick cold butter, cut into
  small dice, plus extra
  for greasing
1 egg, lightly beaten

For the filling
3¼ cups reduced-fat cream
  cheese
2 tablespoons lemon juice
⅓ cup cornstarch
3 eggs, lightly beaten
⅔ cup granulated sugar
2 teaspoons vanilla extract

For the topping
2 cups drained canned dark
  sweet cherries
confectioners' sugar, for dusting

Double Chocolate Cake

Serves 10

Ingredients

*2 sticks butter, softened,
    plus extra for greasing*
1 cup granulated sugar
4 eggs, beaten
1¾ cups all-purpose flour
1¾ teaspoons baking powder
*⅔ cup unsweetened cocoa
    powder*
a little milk (optional)

For the Filling

1 cup heavy cream
*8 ounces white chocolate,
    broken into pieces*

For the Frosting

*12 ounces semisweet chocolate,
    broken into pieces*
1 stick butter
½ cup heavy cream

For the Decoration

*4 ounces semisweet chocolate
    curls*
*2 teaspoons confectioners'
    sugar and unsweetened
    cocoa powder, mixed*

1. To make the filling, put the heavy cream into a saucepan and heat to almost boiling. Put the white chocolate in a food processor and chop. With the motor running, pour the hot cream through the feed tube and process for 10–15 seconds, until smooth. Transfer to a bowl, let cool, then cover with plastic wrap and chill in the refrigerator for 2 hours, or until firm. Beat until just starting to hold soft peaks.

2. Preheat the oven to 350°F. Grease and line the bottom of a deep 8-inch round cake pan. Put the butter and granulated sugar in a bowl and beat until light and fluffy. Gradually beat in the eggs. Sift the flour, baking powder, and cocoa into a bowl, then fold into the mixture, adding milk, if necessary, to make a dropping consistency.

3. Spoon into the prepared pan and bake in the preheated oven for 45–50 minutes, until a toothpick inserted into the center comes out clean. Let stand in the pan for 5 minutes. Transfer to a wire rack to cool completely.

4. To make the frosting, put the semisweet chocolate in a double boiler or a heatproof bowl set over a saucepan of gently simmering water until melted. Stir in the butter and heavy cream. Let cool, stirring occasionally until the mixture is a thick spreading consistency. Slice the cake horizontally into three layers. Sandwich the layers together with the white chocolate filling. Cover the top and sides of the cake with the frosting and arrange the chocolate curls over the top. Sift the mixed confectioners' sugar and cocoa over the cake.

Orange Dessert Cake

1. Preheat the oven to 350°F. Grease and line two 9-inch cake pans.

2. Sift the flour and baking powder into a large bowl and add the butter, granulated sugar, eggs, and orange flower water. Beat well until the mixture is smooth, then stir in the orange juice.

3. Spoon the batter into the prepared pans and smooth the surfaces with a spatula. Bake in the preheated oven for 25–30 minutes, or until risen and golden brown. Let cool in the pans for 5 minutes, then turn out onto a wire rack to cool completely.

4. Beat together all the filling ingredients until smooth, then spread about one-third over one cake. Spoon the remainder into a pastry bag fitted with a large star tip and pipe swirls around the edge of the cake.

5. Place the second cake on top. Pipe the remaining frosting around the top edge. Fill the center with orange slices and brush with maple syrup.

Serves 8–10

Ingredients
oil or melted butter,
  for greasing
1⅓ cup all-purpose flour
1 tablespoon baking powder
1½ sticks unsalted butter,
  softened
¾ cup granulated sugar
3 eggs, beaten
1 teaspoon orange flower water
2 tablespoons orange juice

For the Filling
2½ cups mascarpone cheese
finely grated rind of 1 orange
¼ cup orange juice
½ cup confectioners' sugar
1 teaspoon orange flower water

For the Topping
1 orange, peeled and sliced
maple syrup, for brushing

Walnut Cake

Serves 8–10

Ingredients
oil or melted butter,
  for greasing
1⅓ cups all-purpose flour
1 tablespoon baking powder
1½ sticks unsalted butter,
  softened
¾ cup granulated sugar
3 eggs, beaten
1 teaspoon vanilla extract
2 tablespoons milk
1 cup finely chopped walnuts,
  plus walnut halves to decorate
3 tablespoons apricot
  preserves, warmed

For the Frosting
1½ sticks unsalted butter
2¾ cups confectioners' sugar,
  sifted
½ cup light cream

1. Preheat the oven to 350°F. Grease and line the bottom of two 8-inch cake pans.

2. Sift the flour and baking powder into a large bowl and add the butter, granulated sugar, eggs, and vanilla extract. Beat well until the mixture is smooth, then stir in the milk and ¼ cup of the chopped walnuts.

3. Divide the batter between the prepared pans and smooth the surfaces with a spatula. Bake in the preheated oven for 25–30 minutes, or until risen, firm, and golden brown.

4. Let cool in the pans for 2–3 minutes, then turn out onto a wire rack to cool completely. Slice each cake in half horizontally, to make four layers in total.

5. For the frosting, beat together the butter, confectioners' sugar, and cream until smooth. Spread about half the frosting over the top of three of the cakes and sandwich them together, placing the plain cake on top. Spread half the remaining frosting over the sides of the cake and press the remaining chopped walnuts over it.

6. Brush the apricot preserves over the top of the cake. Spoon the remaining frosting into a pastry bag fitted with a star tip and pipe swirls around the top. Decorate with the walnut halves.

Almond & Hazelnut Cake

1. Preheat the oven to 375°F. Grease two 7-inch cake pans and line with parchment paper.

2. Beat the eggs and granulated sugar in a large mixing bowl with an electric handheld mixer for about 10 minutes, or until the mixture is light and foamy and a trail is left when the beaters are dragged across the surface. Fold in the ground nuts. Sift the flour over the mixture and fold in with a metal spoon or spatula. Divide the batter between the prepared pans.

3. Sprinkle the slivered almonds over the top of one of the cakes. Bake both of the cakes in the preheated oven for 15–20 minutes, or until springy to the touch. Let cool slightly in the pans. Remove the cakes from the pans and transfer to a wire rack to cool completely.

4. Meanwhile, make the filling. Melt the chocolate in a double boiler or a heatproof bowl set over a saucepan of gently simmering water, remove from the heat, and stir in the butter. Let the mixture cool slightly. Whip the cream until just holding its shape, then fold in the melted chocolate mixture.

5. Place the cake without the slivered almonds on a serving plate and spread the filling over it. Let the filling set slightly, then place the almond-topped cake on top and chill for about 1 hour. Dust with confectioners' sugar and serve.

Serves 8

Ingredients
butter, for greasing
4 eggs
⅔ cup granulated sugar
½ cup ground almonds
½ cup ground hazelnuts
⅓ cup all-purpose flour
¾ cup slivered almonds
confectioners' sugar, for dusting

For the Filling
4 ounces semisweet chocolate,
  broken into pieces
1 tablespoon butter
1¼ cups heavy cream

Chocolate & Cherry Cake

Serves 8

Ingredients

oil or melted butter,
  for greasing
1¼ cups all-purpose flour
2 tablespoons unsweetened
  cocoa powder
1 tablespoon baking powder
1½ sticks unsalted butter,
  softened
¾ cup granulated sugar
3 eggs, beaten
1 teaspoon vanilla extract
2 tablespoons milk
3 tablespoons kirsch or brandy
  (optional)
grated chocolate and fresh
  whole sweet cherries,
  to decorate

For the Filling and Topping

2 cups heavy cream
2 tablespoons confectioners'
  sugar
1½ cups pitted fresh dark sweet
  cherries

1. Preheat the oven to 350°F. Grease and line the bottom of two 8-inch cake pans with parchment paper.

2. Sift the flour, cocoa, and baking powder into a large bowl and add the butter, granulated sugar, eggs, and vanilla extract. Beat well until the batter is smooth, then stir in the milk.

3. Divide the batter between the prepared pans and smooth the tops with a spatula. Bake in the preheated oven for 25–30 minutes, or until risen and firm to the touch. Let cool in the pans for 2–3 minutes, then turn out onto a wire rack to cool completely.

4. When the cakes are cold, sprinkle with the kirsch, if using. To make the filling and topping, whip the cream with the confectioners' sugar until thick, then spread about one-third over the top of one of the cakes. Spread the cherries over the cream and place the second cake on top.

5. Spread the remaining cream over the top and sides of the cake and decorate with grated chocolate and fresh whole cherries.

Mississippi Mud Pie

1. Preheat the oven to 350°F. Grease a 9-inch springform or loose-bottom round cake pan.

2. To make the crumb crust, put the cookies, pecans, sugar, and cinnamon into a food processor and process until fine crumbs form; do not overprocess to a powder. Add the melted butter and process again until moistened.

3. Transfer the crumb mixture to the prepared cake pan and press over the bottom and about 1½ inches up the sides of the pan. Cover the pan and chill while you make the filling.

4. To make the filling, put the butter, chocolate, and corn syrup into a saucepan over low heat and stir until melted and blended. Let cool, then beat in the eggs and pecans.

5. Pour the filling into the chilled crust and smooth the surface. Bake in the preheated oven for 30 minutes, or until just set but still soft in the center. Let cool on a wire rack. Serve at room temperature or chilled.

Serves 8

Ingredients

20 graham crackers or
  chocolate cookies
½ cup pecans
1 tablespoon packed light
  brown sugar
½ teaspoon ground cinnamon
6 tablespoons butter, melted

For the Filling

2 sticks butter or margarine,
  plus extra for greasing
6 ounces semisweet chocolate,
  chopped
½ cup light corn syrup
4 extra-large eggs, beaten
¾ cup finely chopped pecans

Meringues!

Meringues are a versatile baking ingredient.
They can be used to decorate cakes and desserts,
and they are also wonderful when eaten on their
own or with a simple cream and preserves filling.

To make 12 small meringues, put 4 egg whites
and a pinch of salt into the bowl of an electric
mixer. Preheat the oven to 250°F and line two
baking sheets with parchment paper. Beat the egg
whites until soft peaks form, then gradually add
1 cup of superfine sugar*. Continue beating until
the mixture is stiff. Put the mixture into a pastry
bag fitted with a plain tip and pipe 12 mounds
onto the prepared baking sheets. Bake in the
preheated oven for about 1½ hours, then turn
off the oven, leaving the meringues inside for
half an hour before serving.

(*To make your own superfine sugar,
blend 1 cup granulated sugar in a
food processor for 1 minute.)

Sachertorte

Serves 10

Ingredients

6 ounces semisweet chocolate,
 broken into pieces
1¼ sticks unsalted butter,
 plus extra for greasing
¾ cup granulated sugar
6 eggs, separated
1⅓ cups all-purpose flour

For the Frosting

8 ounces semisweet chocolate,
 broken into pieces
⅓ cup strong black coffee
1⅓ cups confectioners' sugar
⅓ cup apricot preserves,
 warmed

1. Preheat the oven to 300°F. Grease and line a 9-inch round springform cake pan.

2. Put the chocolate in a heatproof bowl set over a double boiler or a saucepan of gently simmering water until melted. In a separate bowl, beat the butter and ⅓ cup of the sugar until pale and fluffy.

3. Add the egg yolks and beat well. Add the chocolate in a thin stream, beating well. Sift in the flour and fold it into the mixture. Beat the egg whites until they stand in soft peaks. Add the remaining sugar and beat until glossy. Fold half the egg white mixture into the chocolate mixture, then fold in the remainder.

4. Spoon into the prepared pan and smooth the top. Bake in the preheated oven for 1–1¼ hours, until a toothpick inserted into the center comes out clean. Cool in the pan for 5 minutes, then transfer to a wire rack to cool completely.

5. To make the frosting, melt 6 ounces of the chocolate and beat in the coffee until smooth. Sift in the confectioners' sugar and beat to create a thick frosting. Cut the cake horizontally in half. Spread the preserves over the cut edges and sandwich together. Invert the cake on a wire rack. Spoon the frosting over the cake and spread to coat the top and sides. Let set for 5 minutes, letting any excess drop through the rack. Transfer to a serving plate and let set for at least 2 hours.

6. To decorate, melt the remaining chocolate and spoon into a small pastry bag fitted with a fine plain tip. Pipe the word "Sacher" or "Sachertorte" on top of the cake. Let set before serving.

Black Forest Cake

1. Preheat the oven to 400°F. Line an 11-inch round springform cake pan with parchment paper.

2. To make the cake, put the egg whites, water, and salt into a bowl and, using an electric mixer, beat until light and fluffy. Gradually beat in the granulated sugar and continue beating. Mix in the egg yolks and vanilla extract. Sift together the flour, baking powder, and cocoa powder into another bowl, then add to the egg mixture and fold in gently.

3. Pour the batter into the cake pan and bake in the preheated oven for about 20–25 minutes, until risen and just firm to the touch. Turn out onto a wire rack to cool and remove the parchment paper.

4. Cut the cake horizontally into three equal layers. Drizzle 2 tablespoons of the kirsch over each layer.

5. To make the filling, drain the cherries in a strainer, reserving the juice. Bring the cherry juice to a boil in a small saucepan with ½ tablespoon of the granulated sugar. Combine the cornstarch with a little water until dissolved, then stir into the cherry juice until thickened. Add the cherries, remove from the stove, and let cool. Whip the cream with the vanilla extract and the remaining granulated sugar until forming firm peaks.

6. Spread one-third of the whipped cream on the bottom cake layer, then arrange half of the cherries on top. Position the second layer on top, and spread with cream and cherries as above. Finally, place the third layer on top. Spread whipped cream over the whole. Use a spatula to coat the sides of the cake with grated chocolate and sprinkle the rest over the top. Rest in the refrigerator for at least one hour before serving.

Serves 12

Ingredients
6 eggs, separated
⅓ cup warm water
pinch of salt
1 cup granulated sugar
2 teaspoons vanilla extract
2⅓ cups all-purpose flour
2 teaspoons baking powder
1 tablespoon unsweetened
* cocoa powder*
⅓ cup kirsch
2 ounces semisweet chocolate,
* grated, for decorating*

For the filling
2 cups drained canned
* dark sweet cherries*
1½ tablespoons granulated
* sugar*
1 tablespoon cornstarch
2½ cups heavy cream
2 teaspoons vanilla extract

Raspberry & Chocolate Cake

Serves 10

Ingredients

2 sticks butter, plus extra
  for greasing
9 ounces semisweet chocolate
1 tablespoon strong black
  coffee
5 eggs
½ cup granulated sugar
¾ cup all-purpose flour, sifted
1 teaspoon ground cinnamon
1 cup fresh raspberries,
  plus extra to serve
unsweetened cocoa powder,
  for dusting
whipped cream, to serve

1. Preheat the oven to 325°F. Grease a 9-inch round cake pan and line with parchment paper.

2. Put the butter, chocolate, and coffee into a double boiler or a heatproof bowl set over a saucepan of gently simmering water and heat until melted. Stir and let cool slightly.

3. Put the eggs and sugar in a bowl and beat until thick and pale. Gently fold in the chocolate mixture. Sift the flour and cinnamon into a bowl, then fold into the chocolate mixture. Pour into the prepared pan and sprinkle the raspberries evenly over the top.

4. Bake in the preheated oven for 35–45 minutes, until the cake is well risen and springy to the touch. Let cool in the pan for 15 minutes before turning out onto a large plate. Dust with cocoa and serve with raspberries and whipped cream.

Citrus Mousse Cake

1. Preheat the oven to 350°F. Grease and line the bottom of an 8-inch round springform cake pan.

2. Beat the butter and sugar in a bowl until light and fluffy. Gradually add the eggs, beating well after each addition. Sift the flour, baking powder, and cocoa over the mixture and fold in. Fold in the melted chocolate.

3. Pour into the prepared pan and level the top. Bake in the preheated oven for 40 minutes, or until springy to the touch. Let cool for 5 minutes in the pan, then turn out onto a wire rack and let cool completely. Cut the cold cake horizontally into two layers.

4. To make the orange mousse, beat the egg yolks and sugar until pale, then beat in the orange juice. Sprinkle the gelatin over the water in a small heatproof bowl and let it turn spongy, then put over a saucepan of hot water and stir until dissolved. Stir into the egg yolk mixture. Whip the cream until holding its shape, reserve a little for decoration, then fold the remainder into the orange mixture. Beat the egg whites until standing in soft peaks, then fold in. Let stand in a cool place until starting to set, stirring occasionally.

5. Place half of the cake back in the pan. Pour in the mousse and press the second cake layer on top. Chill until set. Transfer to a serving plate, spoon teaspoonfuls of cream around the top, and decorate the center with orange segments.

Serves 8

Ingredients
1½ sticks butter, plus extra
   for greasing
¾ cup granulated sugar
4 eggs, lightly beaten
1⅔ cups all-purpose flour
1½ teaspoons baking powder
1 tablespoon unsweetened
   cocoa powder
2 ounces orange-flavored
   semisweet chocolate, melted
peeled orange segments,
   to decorate

For the Orange Mousse
2 eggs, separated
¼ cup granulated sugar
1 cup freshly squeezed
   orange juice
2 teaspoons powdered gelatin
3 tablespoons water
1¼ cups heavy cream

Small Baked Goods and Breads

Classic Vanilla Cupcakes

Makes 12

Ingredients

1½ sticks unsalted butter, softened
¾ cup granulated sugar
3 extra-large eggs, beaten
1 teaspoon vanilla extract
1⅓ cups all-purpose flour
1¼ teaspoons baking powder
sprinkles, to decorate

For the Frosting

1¼ sticks unsalted butter, softened
3 tablespoons heavy cream or milk
1 teaspoon vanilla extract
2⅓ cups confectioners' sugar, sifted

1. Preheat the oven to 350°F. Place 12 paper liners in a muffin pan.

2. Put the butter and granulated sugar into a bowl and beat together until pale and creamy. Gradually beat in the eggs and vanilla extract. Sift in the flour and baking powder and fold in gently.

3. Divide the batter evenly among the paper liners and bake in the preheated oven for 15–20 minutes, or until risen and firm to the touch. Transfer to a wire rack and let cool.

4. To make the frosting, put the butter into a bowl and beat with an electric mixer for 2–3 minutes, or until pale and creamy. Beat in the cream and vanilla extract. Gradually beat in the confectioners' sugar and continue beating until the frosting is light and fluffy.

5. Use a spatula to swirl the frosting over the tops of the cupcakes. Decorate with sprinkles.

Chocolate & Nut Cakes

1. Preheat the oven to 350°F. Grease four tall ovenproof ramekins (ceramic dishes) or molds.

2. To make the cakes, use an electric mixer or a wooden spoon to beat the butter in a large bowl until light and fluffy, gradually add the confectioners' sugar, and beat thoroughly. Break the ladyfingers into pieces and stir into the butter mixture together with the hazelnuts and grated chocolate. Add the egg yolks, brandy, and Crème de Cacao and mix well.

3. Beat the egg whites until they hold stiff peaks, fold carefully into the batter, and divide evenly among the molds. Cover with greased aluminum foil.

4. Place the molds in a roasting pan and pour in hot water to halfway up the ramekins. Carefully place in the preheated oven and bake for about 45 minutes, until the batter has set.

5. To make the sauce, put the water, sugar, and orange juice and rind into a small saucepan and bring to a boil. Reduce the heat and simmer for 3 minutes. Break the chocolate into small pieces and put in a double boiler or a heatproof bowl set over a saucepan of gently simmering water. Melt the chocolate, stirring continuously, then slowly stir in the orange syrup.

6. Use a knife to help ease the cakes out of the molds and turn out onto plates. Pour the sauce over the cakes and serve warm.

Makes 4

Ingredients
*4 tablespoons butter, plus extra
  for greasing
3 tablespoons confectioners'
  sugar
4 ladyfingers
¼ cup ground hazelnuts
2 ounces semisweet chocolate,
  grated
2 eggs, separated
1 tablespoon brandy
1 tablespoon Crème de Cacao*

For the Sauce
*4 teaspoons water
2½ tablespoons granulated sugar
juice and grated rind of 1 orange
4 ounces semisweet chocolate*

Cinnamon Swirls

Makes 12

Ingredients

1⅔ cups white bread flour
½ teaspoon salt
2¼ teaspoons active dry yeast
2 tablespoons butter, cut into
 small pieces, plus extra for
 greasing
1 egg, lightly beaten
½ cup lukewarm milk
2 tablespoons maple syrup,
 for glazing

For the Filling

4 tablespoons butter, softened
2 teaspoons ground cinnamon
¼ cup firmly packed light
 brown sugar
⅓ cup dried currants

1. Grease a baking sheet and a bowl. Sift the flour and salt into a mixing bowl and stir in the yeast.

2. Rub in the chopped butter with your fingertips until the mixture resembles bread crumbs. Add the egg and milk and mix to form a dough.

3. Form the dough into a ball, place in the greased bowl, cover, and let stand in a warm place for about 40 minutes, or until doubled in volume.

4. Knead the dough for 1 minute, then roll out to a rectangle measuring 12 x 19 inches.

5. For the filling, cream together the softened butter, cinnamon, and sugar until light and fluffy.

6. Spread the filling over the dough, leaving a 1-inch border. Sprinkle the currants evenly over the top. Roll up the dough from one of the long edges and press down to seal.

7. Preheat the oven to 375°F. Cut the roll into 12 slices and place them, cut side down, on the prepared baking sheet. Cover and let stand for 30 minutes.

8. Bake in the preheated oven for 20–30 minutes, or until the swirls are well risen.

9. Brush with maple syrup and let cool slightly before serving.

Cherry Tarts

1. Preheat the oven to 375°F. Put the flour, confectioners' sugar, cinnamon, and butter into a food processor and process until evenly blended.

2. Add the egg yolk and water to the mixture, and blend until it just binds to form a soft dough.

3. Divide the dough into four and press into four 4-inch loose-bottom tart pans, pressing with your knuckles to spread evenly.

4. Place on a baking sheet and bake the crusts for 12–15 minutes, then remove from the oven and let cool. Stir the cherries into the yogurt and spoon into the pastry shells.

5. Drizzle the tarts with honey, sprinkle with cinnamon, and serve with whole cherries.

Makes 4

Ingredients
1 cup all-purpose flour, sifted
2 tablespoons confectioners' sugar, sifted
½ teaspoon ground cinnamon
5 tablespoons unsalted butter, at room temperature
1 egg yolk
2 tablespoons cold water

For the Filling
2⅓ cups pitted dark sweet cherries
⅔ cup Greek-style yogurt
2 tablespoons honey
cinnamon and whole sweet cherries, to decorate

Vanilla Whoopie Pies

Makes 12

Ingredients
2 cups all-purpose flour
1 teaspoon baking soda
large pinch of salt
1½ sticks butter, softened
¾ cup granulated sugar
1 extra-large egg, beaten
2 teaspoons vanilla extract
⅔ cup buttermilk

For the Chocolate Filling
4 ounces milk chocolate,
  broken into pieces
1 stick unsalted butter, softened
2 cups confectioners' sugar,
  sifted

1. Preheat the oven to 350°F. Line two to three large baking sheets with parchment paper. Sift together the all-purpose flour, baking soda, and salt.

2. Put the butter and sugar into a large bowl and beat with an electric handheld mixer until pale and fluffy. Beat in the egg and vanilla extract, followed by half the flour mixture and then the buttermilk. Stir in the rest of the flour mixture and mix until thoroughly incorporated.

3. Pipe or spoon 24 mounds of the batter onto the prepared baking sheets, spaced well apart to allow for spreading. Bake in the preheated oven, one sheet at a time, for 10–12 minutes, or until risen and just firm to the touch. Cool for 5 minutes, then, using a spatula, transfer to a wire rack and let cool completely.

4. For the filling, put the chocolate in a double boiler or a heatproof bowl set over a saucepan of simmering water and heat until melted. Remove from the heat and let cool for 20 minutes, stirring occasionally. Place the butter in a bowl and beat with an electric mixer for 2–3 minutes, or until pale and creamy. Gradually beat in the confectioners' sugar, then beat in the chocolate.

5. To assemble, spread or pipe the chocolate filling on the flat side of half of the cakes. Top with the rest of the cakes.

Cinnamon Waffles

1. Melt the butter in a small saucepan. Sift the flour into a bowl and gradually stir in the cream, egg yolks, spices, vanilla seeds, and 2½ tablespoons of the melted butter.

2. Put the egg whites and half of the sugar in a bowl and beat until light and fluffy. Gradually add the remaining sugar and continue beating until the whipped egg white forms firm peaks. Fold one-third of the egg white into the cream mixture, then mix in the rest.

3. Preheat the waffle maker and grease lightly with butter.

4. Pour a little batter into the waffle maker, spread out, and cook the waffle on medium heat until golden brown. Continue cooking all of the waffles until the batter is used.

5. Brush the waffles with the remaining melted butter and sprinkle with sugar.

Makes 8

Ingredients
1 stick butter, plus extra
   for greasing
¾ cup all-purpose flour
⅔ cup light cream
2 egg yolks
½ teaspoon cinnamon
pinch of ground cloves
seeds from 1 vanilla bean
3 egg whites
2 tablespoons granulated sugar,
   plus extra for sprinkling

Apple Fritters

Makes 12

Ingredients
2⅓ cups all-purpose flour
1½ tablespoons baking powder
⅓ cup granulated sugar
1½ cups milk
3 eggs, separated
4 apples
juice of ½ lemon
vegetable oil, for frying
confectioners' sugar, for dusting

For the Sauce
1 vanilla bean
1 cup milk
6 eggs yolks
¼ cup granulated sugar

1. Sift the flour and baking powder into a large bowl, add the sugar, milk, and egg yolks, and mix to a smooth batter. Beat the egg whites until holding firm peaks and carefully fold into the batter.

2. Peel the apples and remove the core with a corer. Cut them horizontally into ¼-inch-thick slices and rub them with the lemon juice to prevent them from browning.

3. Pour the vegetable oil into a saucepan and heat to 325°F or until a little of the batter dropped into the hot oil bubbles and rises to the surface immediately.

4. Coat the apple slices with batter, carefully add to the hot oil immediately, a few at a time, and cook until the apple slices are golden brown. Drain thoroughly on paper towels, then dust with the confectioners' sugar and keep warm while you make the sauce.

5. To make the sauce, cut the vanilla bean in half lengthwise and scrape out the seeds. Pour the milk into a saucepan, add the vanilla seeds and the bean and bring to a boil. Meanwhile, beat the egg yolks with the sugar in a bowl until light and fluffy. Remove the vanilla bean from the hot milk and pour into the egg-and-sugar mixture, stirring continuously. Return to the pan and heat gently for a few minutes, stirring all the time, until just thickened. Pour into a pitcher and serve warm or cold with the fritters.

It's the love and care put into each batch of cakes that gives the most joy to those who eat them, and to you as the cook.

Apple Danish

1. Put the flour into a bowl and rub in 2 tablespoons of the butter. Set aside. Dust the remaining butter with flour, grate coarsely into a bowl, and chill. Stir the salt, yeast, and sugar into the flour mixture.

2. In another bowl, beat the egg with the vanilla extract and water, add to the flour mixture, and mix to form a dough. Knead for 10 minutes on a floured surface, then chill for 10 minutes.

3. Roll out the dough to a 12 x 8-inch rectangle. Mark widthwise into thirds and fold. Press the edges with a rolling pin and roll out to the same size as the original rectangle.

4. Sprinkle the grated butter evenly over the top two-thirds. Fold up the bottom third and fold down the top third. Press the edges, wrap in plastic wrap, and chill for 30 minutes. Repeat four times, chilling well each time. Chill overnight.

5. Mix together the filling ingredients. Preheat the oven to 400°F. Grease two baking sheets.

6. Roll out the dough into a 16-inch square and cut into 16 squares. Pile some filling in the center of each, reserving any juice. Brush the edges of the squares with milk and bring the corners together in the center.

7. Place on the prepared baking sheets and chill for 15 minutes. Brush with the reserved juice and sprinkle with granulated sugar.

8. Bake in the preheated oven for 10 minutes, reduce the temperature to 350°F, and bake for an additional 10–15 minutes, until browned.

9. Gently remove from the baking sheets and serve.

Makes 12–16

Ingredients
2 cups white bread flour,
  plus extra, sifted, for dusting
1½ sticks butter, well chilled,
  plus extra for greasing
½ teaspoon salt
2¼ teaspoons active dry yeast
2 tablespoons granulated sugar,
  plus extra for sprinkling
1 egg
1 teaspoon vanilla extract
⅓ cup lukewarm water
milk, for glazing

For the Filling
2 Pippin or other sweet crisp
  apples, peeled, cored,
  and chopped
grated rind of 1 lemon
3 tablespoons sugar

Blueberry Muffins

Makes 12

Ingredients

2¼ cups all-purpose flour
1 tablespoon baking powder
pinch of salt
½ cup firmly packed light
    brown sugar
1 cup frozen blueberries
2 eggs
1 cup milk
6 tablespoons butter, melted
    and cooled
1 teaspoon vanilla extract
finely grated rind of 1 lemon

1. Preheat the oven to 400°F. Place 12 muffin cups in a muffin pan. Sift the flour, baking powder, and salt into a large bowl. Stir in the sugar and blueberries.

2. Lightly beat the eggs in a small bowl, then beat in the milk, melted butter, vanilla extract, and lemon rind. Make a well in the center of the dry ingredients and pour in the liquid ingredients. Stir gently until just combined; do not overmix.

3. Divide the batter evenly among the muffin cups. Bake in the preheated oven for about 20 minutes, or until well risen, golden brown, and firm to the touch.

4. Let the muffins cool in the pan for 5 minutes, then serve warm or transfer to a wire rack and let cool.

Chocolate & Orange Muffins

1. Preheat the oven to 400°F. Place 12 muffin cups in a muffin pan.

2. Finely grate the rind from the oranges and squeeze the juice. Add enough milk to make up the juice to 1 cup, then add the orange rind. Sift the flour, cocoa, baking powder, and salt into a large bowl. Stir in the brown sugar and chocolate chips. Put the eggs into a small bowl and beat lightly, then beat in the milk-and-orange mixture and the oil. Make a well in the center of the dry ingredients and pour in the liquid ingredients. Stir gently until just combined; do not overmix. Divide the batter evenly among the muffin cups.

3. Bake in the preheated oven for 20 minutes, or until well risen and firm to the touch. Let cool in the pan for 5 minutes, then transfer to a wire rack to cool completely.

4. To make the frosting, put the chocolate, butter, and water into a double boiler or a heatproof bowl set over a saucepan of gently simmering water and heat, stirring, until melted. Remove from the heat and sift in the confectioners' sugar. Beat until smooth, then spread the frosting on top of the muffins and decorate with strips of orange zest.

Makes 12

Ingredients
2 oranges
about ½ cup milk
1¾ cups all-purpose flour
⅔ cup unsweetened cocoa
* powder*
1 tablespoon baking powder
pinch of salt
½ cup firmly packed light
* brown sugar*
1 cup semisweet chocolate
* chips*
2 eggs
⅓ cup sunflower oil or
* 6 tablespoons butter, melted*
* and cooled*
strips of orange zest,
* to decorate*

For the Frosting
2 ounces semisweet chocolate,
* broken into pieces*
2 tablespoons butter
2 tablespoons water
1⅓ cups confectioners' sugar

Blueberry Cream Puffs

Makes 12

Ingredients
½ cup milk
4 tablespoons butter
1 cup all-purpose flour
pinch of salt
3 eggs, beaten

For the Filling
1¼ cups heavy cream
2 cups blueberries
2 tablespoons granulated sugar
1 teaspoon lemon juice
⅓ cup blackberries
confectioners' sugar, for dusting

1. Preheat the oven to 400°F. Line a baking sheet with parchment paper.

2. To make the pastry dough, put the milk and butter into a medium saucepan and bring to a boil. Add the flour and salt and, using a wooden spoon, beat thoroughly until a smooth ball of dough has formed. Let cool for 10–15 minutes.

3. Use a wooden spoon to beat the eggs, a little at a time, into the dough (it may not all be needed) to form a smooth, glossy paste. Spoon the dough into a pastry bag fitted with a large star-shape tip and pipe about 12 balls (2 inches in diameter) onto the prepared baking sheet. Bake in the preheated oven for about 20–25 minutes. Place a baking sheet sprinkled with hot water on the floor of the oven to help the cream puffs rise better. Let the cream puffs cool and cut in half horizontally.

4. To make the filling, whip the cream until holding stiff peaks. Process 1½ cups of the blueberries with the granulated sugar and lemon juice and gently fold into the cream. Spoon the cream filling into a pastry bag with a large tip and pipe onto the lower halves of the cream puffs. Sprinkle the remaining blueberries and the blackberries on top. Put the top halves into position and dust with the confectioners' sugar to serve.

Cinnamon Orange Fritters

1. Sift the flour into a bowl and stir in the yeast and sugar.

2. Add the milk, egg, orange rind, flower water, and butter and mix to a soft dough, kneading until smooth.

3. Cover and let stand in a warm place until doubled in volume. Roll out on a lightly floured surface to a thickness of ½ inch, then cut into eight 3-inch squares.

4. Heat the oil to 350°F. Fry the fritters, in batches, until golden brown. Remove with a slotted spoon and drain on paper towels.

5. Sprinkle with cinnamon sugar and serve hot with orange slices or segments.

Makes 8

Ingredients
2 cups all-purpose flour
1 teaspoon active dry yeast
1½ tablespoons granulated
   sugar
½ cup lukewarm milk
1 egg, beaten
finely grated rind of
   1 small orange
1 teaspoon orange flower water
3 tablespoons butter, melted
sunflower oil, for deep-frying
cinnamon sugar, for dusting
orange slices or segments,
   to serve

Summer Fruit Tarts

Makes 12

Ingredients

1⅔ cups all-purpose flour,
   plus extra for dusting
⅔ cup confectioners' sugar,
   sifted
½ cup ground almonds
1 stick butter
1 egg yolk
1 tablespoon milk

For the Filling

1 cup cream cheese
confectioners' sugar, to taste,
   plus extra, sifted, for dusting
2⅓ cups fresh summer
   berries, such as raspberries,
   blueberries, and halved or
   quartered strawberries

1. Sift the flour and confectioners' sugar into a bowl. Stir in the almonds. Add the butter, rubbing in until the mixture resembles bread crumbs. Add the egg yolk and milk and work in until the dough binds together. Wrap in plastic wrap and chill for 30 minutes.

2. Preheat the oven to 400°F. Roll out the dough on a lightly floured surface and use it to line 12 individual deep tart pans. Prick the bottoms and press a piece of aluminum foil into each.

3. Bake in the preheated oven for 10–15 minutes, or until light golden brown. Remove the foil and bake for an additional 2–3 minutes. Transfer to a wire rack to cool.

4. For the filling, put the cream cheese and confectioners' sugar in a bowl and mix together. Place a spoonful of filling in each tart and arrange the berries on top.

5. Dust with sifted confectioners' sugar and serve immediately.

Sugar Cookies

1. Put the butter and sugar into a bowl and beat together until pale and creamy. Beat in the lemon rind and egg yolk. Sift in the flour and mix to a soft dough. Turn out onto a floured work surface and knead until smooth, adding a little more flour, if necessary. Halve the dough, shape into balls, wrap in plastic wrap, and chill in the refrigerator for 1 hour.

2. Preheat the oven to 350°F and lightly grease two large baking sheets.

3. Roll out the dough on a lightly floured work surface to a thickness of ¼ inch. Using 2¾-inch flower-shape and heart-shape cutters, stamp out 20 cookies, rerolling the dough as necessary. Place on the prepared baking sheets and sprinkle with sugar.

4. Bake in the preheated oven for 10–12 minutes, or until pale golden brown. Let cool on the baking sheets for 2–3 minutes, then transfer to a wire rack to cool completely.

Makes 20

Ingredients

*1 stick butter, softened,
    plus extra for greasing*
*¼ cup granulated sugar,
    plus extra for sprinkling*
*1 teaspoon finely grated
    lemon rind*
1 egg yolk
*1⅓ cups all-purpose flour,
    plus extra for dusting*

Chocolate Chip Cookies

Makes 8

Ingredients

unsalted butter, melted,
*   for greasing*
1⅓ cups all-purpose flour,
*   sifted*
1 teaspoon baking powder
1 stick or ½ cup margarine,
*   melted*
⅓ cup firmly packed light
*   brown sugar*
¼ cup granulated sugar
½ teaspoon vanilla extract
1 egg, beaten
⅔ cup semisweet chocolate
*   chips*

1. Preheat the oven to 375°F. Lightly grease two baking sheets.

2. Put all of the ingredients into a large mixing bowl and beat until well combined.

3. Place tablespoons of the dough on the prepared baking sheets, spaced well apart.

4. Bake in the preheated oven for 10–12 minutes, or until golden brown. Transfer to a wire rack and let cool.

Snickerdoodles

1. Preheat the oven to 350°F. Line two large baking sheets with parchment paper.

2. Put the butter and granulated sugar into a bowl and beat together until pale and creamy. Gradually beat in the egg and vanilla extract. Sift in the flour and baking powder and mix to a smooth dough.

3. Mix together the granulated sugar and cinnamon on a plate. Divide the dough into 24 even pieces and shape each piece into a walnut-size ball. Roll the balls in the cinnamon sugar, then place on the prepared baking sheets, spaced well apart to allow for spreading. Flatten each ball slightly with your fingers.

4. Bake in the preheated oven for 12–14 minutes, or until golden brown. Let cool on the baking sheets for 5 minutes, then transfer to a wire rack to cool completely.

Makes 24

Ingredients
6 tablespoons butter, softened
¾ cup granulated sugar
1 extra-large egg, beaten
½ teaspoon vanilla extract
2 cups all-purpose flour
1 teaspoon baking powder
3 tablespoons granulated sugar
1 tablespoon ground cinnamon

Marzipan Ring Cakes

Makes 8

Ingredients

1 stick unsalted butter, softened
2½ tablespoons granulated
  sugar
½ teaspoon almond extract
1 cup all-purpose flour, sifted
1 tablespoon milk (optional)
1½ ounces marzipan
4 teaspoons apricot preserves,
  warmed
confectioners' sugar, sifted,
  for dusting

1. Preheat the oven to 375°F. Put eight paper liners in a shallow muffin pan.

2. Put the butter, granulated sugar, and almond extract into a food processor and process until pale and fluffy. Add the flour and process to a soft dough, adding milk, if necessary. Spoon the batter into a pastry bag fitted with a large star tip. Pipe the batter in a spiral around the sides of each paper liner, leaving a dip in the center. Cut the marzipan into eight cubes and press one into the center of each whirl.

3. Bake in the preheated oven for 15–20 minutes, until pale and golden brown. Lift the cakes onto a wire rack to cool. Once the cakes have cooled, spoon a little of the apricot preserves into the center of each. Dust the cakes with confectioners' sugar, and serve.

Crown Loaf

1. Grease a baking sheet. Sift the flour and salt into a bowl. Stir in the yeast. Rub in the diced butter with your fingertips. Add the milk and egg and mix to form a dough.

2. Place the dough in a greased bowl, cover, and let stand in a warm place for 40 minutes, or until doubled in volume.

3. Knead for 1 minute. Roll out to a 12 x 9-inch rectangle.

4. For the filling, cream the butter and sugar until light and fluffy. Stir in the hazelnuts, ginger, candied peel, and rum.

5. Spread the filling over the dough, leaving a 1-inch border.

6. Roll up the dough, starting from one of the long edges, into a log shape. Cut into slices at 2-inch intervals and place in a circle on the prepared baking sheet with the slices just touching.

7. Cover and let stand in a warm place for 30 minutes. Meanwhile, preheat the oven to 375°F. Bake the loaf in the preheated oven for 20–30 minutes, or until golden brown.

8. For the icing, mix the sugar with enough lemon juice to form a thin icing. Let the loaf cool slightly before drizzling with the icing. Let the icing set before cutting into nine pieces and serving.

Serves 9

Ingredients
1⅔ cups white bread flour
½ teaspoon salt
2¼ teaspoons active dry yeast
2 tablespoons butter, diced,
  plus extra for greasing
½ cup lukewarm milk
1 egg, lightly beaten

For the Filling
4 tablespoons butter, softened
¼ cup firmly packed light
  brown sugar
2 tablespoons chopped
  hazelnuts
1 tablespoon crystallized ginger
¼ cup chopped candied peel
1 tablespoon dark rum
  or brandy

For the Icing
1 cup confectioners' sugar,
  sifted
1–2 tablespoons lemon juice

Poppy Seed Braid

Makes 1 Loaf

Ingredients

1⅔ cups white bread flour,
  plus extra for dusting
1 teaspoon salt
2 tablespoons instant skim milk
1½ tablespoons granulated
  sugar
1 teaspoon active dry yeast
¾ cup lukewarm water
2 tablespoons vegetable oil,
  plus extra for greasing
⅓ cup poppy seeds

For the Topping

1 egg yolk
1 tablespoon milk
1 tablespoon granulated sugar
2 tablespoons poppy seeds

1. Sift the flour and salt into a bowl and stir in the instant milk, sugar, and yeast. Make a well in the center, pour in the water and oil, and stir until the dough begins to come together.

2. Add the poppy seeds and knead until fully combined and the dough leaves the side of the bowl. Turn out onto a lightly floured surface and knead well for about 10 minutes, until smooth and elastic.

3. Brush a bowl with oil. Shape the dough into a ball, put it in the bowl, cover, and let rise in a warm place for 1 hour, or until doubled in volume.

4. Oil a baking sheet. Turn out the dough onto a lightly floured surface, punch down to knock out the air, and knead for 1–2 minutes. Divide into three equal pieces and shape each into a rope 10–12 inches long.

5. Place the ropes side by side and press together at one end. Braid the dough, pinch the other end together, and tuck underneath.

6. Put the loaf on the prepared baking sheet, cover, and let rise in a warm place for 30 minutes. Meanwhile, preheat the oven to 400°F.

7. For the topping, beat the egg yolk with the milk and sugar. Brush the egg glaze over the top of the loaf and sprinkle with the poppy seeds.

8. Bake in the preheated oven for 30–35 minutes, until golden brown. Transfer to a wire rack and let cool.

9. Serve plain or toasted as a lunchtime treat.

Whole-Wheat Loaf

1. Put the flour, instant milk, salt, sugar, and yeast into a large bowl. Pour in the oil and add the water, then mix well to make a smooth dough.

2. Turn out onto a lightly floured surface and knead well for about 10 minutes, or until smooth. Brush a bowl with oil. Shape the dough into a ball, put it into the bowl, and cover with a damp dish towel. Let rise in a warm place for 1 hour, or until the dough has doubled in volume.

3. Preheat the oven to 425°F. Oil a 9-inch loaf pan. Turn the dough out onto a lightly floured surface and knead for 1 minute, or until smooth. Shape the dough the length of the pan and three times the width. Fold the dough into three widthwise and place it in the pan with the seam underneath. Cover and let stand in a warm place for 30 minutes, or until it has risen above the pan.

4. Place in the preheated oven and bake for 30 minutes, or until firm and golden brown. Test that the loaf is cooked by tapping on the bottom with your knuckles—it should sound hollow. Transfer to a wire rack to cool. Serve with cheese and a relish of your choice.

Makes 1 Loaf

Ingredients:
1⅔ cups whole-wheat bread
  flour, plus extra for dusting
1 tablespoon instant skim milk
1 teaspoon salt
2 tablespoons packed light
  brown sugar
1 teaspoon active dry yeast
1½ tablespoons sunflower oil,
  plus extra for greasing
¾ cup lukewarm water
cheese and relish, to serve

White Crusty Loaf

Makes 1 Loaf

Ingredients

1 egg
1 egg yolk
⅔–1 cup lukewarm water
3⅔ cups white bread flour,
    sifted, plus extra for dusting
1½ teaspoons salt
2 teaspoons sugar
1 teaspoon active dry yeast
2 tablespoons butter, diced
oil, for greasing

1. Put the egg and egg yolk into a liquid measuring cup and beat lightly to mix. Add enough water to make up to 1¼ cups, Stir well.

2. Put the flour, salt, sugar, and yeast into a large bowl. Add the butter and rub it in with your fingertips until the mixture resembles fine bread crumbs.

3. Make a well in the center, add the egg mixture, and work to a smooth dough. Turn out onto a lightly floured surface and knead well for about 10 minutes, until smooth.

4. Brush a bowl with oil. Shape the dough into a ball, put into the bowl, cover, and let rise in a warm place for 1 hour, or until doubled in volume.

5. Preheat the oven to 425°F. Oil a 9-inch loaf pan. Turn out the dough onto a lightly floured surface and knead for 1 minute, until smooth.

6. Shape the dough so it is the same length as the loaf pan and three times the width. Fold the dough in three widthwise and put it into the pan with the seam underneath.

7. Cover and let stand in a warm place for 30 minutes, until the dough has risen above the pan.

8. Put into the preheated oven and bake for 30 minutes, or until firm and golden brown. Transfer to a wire rack and let cool.

9. Cut into thick slices and serve.

Mixed Seed Bread

1. Put the flours, instant milk, salt, sugar, and yeast into a large bowl. Pour in the oil and add the lemon juice and water. Stir in the seeds and mix well to make a smooth dough. Turn out onto a lightly floured surface and knead well for about 10 minutes, until smooth.

2. Brush a bowl with oil. Shape the dough into a ball, put it into the bowl, and cover with a damp dish towel. Let rise in a warm place for 1 hour, until the dough has doubled in volume. Oil a 9-inch loaf pan. Turn out the dough onto a lightly floured surface and knead for 1 minute, until smooth. Shape the dough to the length of the pan and three times the width. Fold the dough in three widthwise and put it into the pan with the seam underneath. Cover and let stand in a warm place for 30 minutes, until it has risen above the pan.

3. Preheat the oven to 425°F. For the topping, lightly beat the egg white with the water to make a glaze. Just before baking, brush the glaze over the loaf, then gently press the sunflower seeds all over the top.

4. Bake in the preheated oven for 30 minutes, or until firm and golden brown. Test that the loaf is cooked by tapping on the bottom with your knuckles—it should sound hollow. Transfer to a wire rack to cool.

Makes 1 Loaf

Ingredients
2¾ cups white bread flour,
  plus extra for dusting
1 cup rye flour
1½ tablespoons instant
  skim milk
1½ teaspoons salt
1 tablespoon packed light
  brown sugar
1 teaspoon active dry yeast
1½ tablespoons sunflower oil,
  plus extra for greasing
2 teaspoons lemon juice
1¼ cups lukewarm water
1 teaspoon caraway seeds
½ teaspoon poppy seeds
½ teaspoon sesame seeds

For the Topping
1 egg white
1 tablespoon water
1 tablespoon sunflower seeds
  or pumpkin seeds

Rye Bread

Makes 1 Loaf

Ingredients

3½ cups rye flour
1⅔ cups white bread flour,
    plus extra for dusting
2 teaspoons salt
2 teaspoons packed light
    brown sugar
1½ teaspoons active dry yeast
2 cups lukewarm water
2 teaspoons vegetable oil,
    plus extra for greasing
1 egg white

1. Sift the flours and salt into a bowl. Add the sugar and yeast and stir to mix. Make a well in the center and pour in the water and oil.

2. Stir until the dough begins to come together, then knead until it leaves the side of the bowl. Turn out onto a lightly floured surface and knead for 10 minutes, until elastic and smooth.

3. Brush a bowl with oil. Shape the dough into a ball, put it in the bowl, cover, and let rise in a warm place for 2 hours, or until doubled in volume.

4. Oil a baking sheet. Turn out the dough onto a lightly floured surface and punch down to knock out the air, then knead for 10 minutes.

5. Shape the dough into a ball, put it on the prepared baking sheet, and cover. Let rise in a warm place for an additional 40 minutes, or until doubled in volume.

6. Meanwhile, preheat the oven to 375°F. Beat the egg white with 1 tablespoon of water in a bowl.

7. Bake the loaf in the preheated oven for 20 minutes, then remove from the oven and brush the top with the egg white glaze. Return to the oven and bake for an additional 20 minutes.

8. Brush the top of the loaf with the glaze again and return to the oven for an additional 20–30 minutes, until the crust is a rich brown. Transfer to a wire rack to cool.

9. Serve with good quality butter or a topping of your choice.

Christmas
Treats

Stollen

Makes 1 stollen

Ingredients
⅔ cup lukewarm milk
¼ cup granulated sugar
2 teaspoons active dry yeast
2½ cups white bread flour,
   plus extra for dusting
½ teaspoon salt
1 stick softened butter,
   plus extra for greasing
1 egg, beaten
⅓ cup dried currants
⅓ cup golden raisins
¼ cup candied lemon peel
¼ cup candied cherries
¼ cup chopped almonds
grated rind of ½ lemon
6 ounces marzipan
confectioners' sugar, for dusting

1. To make the stollen dough, put the milk and one teaspoon of the sugar in a bowl, sprinkle in the yeast, and stir, or follow package directions. Let stand in a warm place until frothy.

2. Sift the flour and salt into a bowl and add the remaining sugar. Make a well in the center. Pour in the yeast mixture. Add the butter and egg and mix to a smooth dough. Knead for 5–6 minutes, until smooth and elastic.

3. Knead the currants, golden raisins, lemon peel, cherries, almonds, and lemon rind into the dough. Cover the bowl and let rise in a warm place for 2 hours, until the dough has doubled in volume.

4. Turn the dough out onto a floured surface and knead for 2–3 minutes. Break up the marzipan or cut it into small pieces and knead into the dough.

5. Roll the dough into a cylinder shape. Grease a baking sheet and place the stollen on it. Cover with a cloth and let rise again until it has doubled in volume. Preheat the oven to 375°F.

6. Bake the stollen for about 40 minutes, or until golden brown. Place on a wire rack and let cool completely. Dust with plenty of confectioners' sugar to serve.

Lebkuchen

1. Preheat the oven to 350°F. Line several baking sheets with parchment paper.

2. Put the eggs and sugar into a double boiler or a heatproof bowl set over a saucepan of gently simmering water. Beat until thick and foamy. Remove from the heat and continue to beat for 2 minutes.

3. Sift the flour, cocoa powder, cinnamon, cardamom, cloves, and nutmeg into the bowl and stir in with the ground almonds and candied peel. Drop heaping teaspoonfuls of the batter onto the prepared baking sheets, spreading them gently into smooth mounds.

4. Bake in the preheated oven for 15–20 minutes, until light brown and slightly soft to the touch. Cool on the baking sheets for 10 minutes, then transfer to wire racks to cool completely.

5. Put the semisweet and white chocolate in two separate double boilers or heatproof bowls set over two saucepans of gently simmering water until melted. Dip half the cookies in the melted semisweet chocolate and half in the white chocolate. Sprinkle with sugar crystals and let set.

Makes 60

Ingredients
3 eggs
1 cup granulated sugar
⅓ cup all-purpose flour
2 teaspoons unsweetened
  cocoa powder
1 teaspoon ground cinnamon
½ teaspoon ground cardamom
¼ teaspoon ground cloves
¼ teaspoon ground nutmeg
1¾ cups ground almonds
  (almond meal)
¼ cup finely chopped
  candied peel

For the Decoration
4 ounces semisweet chocolate
4 ounces white chocolate
sugar crystals

Spiced Citrus Cookies

Makes 65

Ingredients
2 eggs
1¼ cups granulated sugar
pinch of salt
⅓ cup finely chopped candied
  orange peel
grated rind of ½ lemon
2⅓ cups all-purpose flour,
  plus extra for dusting
2 tablespoons ground allspice
½ teaspoon baking powder
1 tablespoon water

1. To make the dough, put the eggs, sugar, and salt into a bowl and beat with a wire whisk until light and frothy. In a separate bowl, mix together the orange peel, lemon rind, flour, and half of the allspice.

2. Dissolve the baking powder in the water and stir into the egg mixture, then gradually fold in the flour mixture to make a firm dough. Cover and chill in the refrigerator for 3–4 hours or overnight.

3. Preheat the oven to 400°F. Line two large baking sheets with parchment paper.

4. Turn the cookie dough out onto a floured surface. Knead gently until smooth, then, using floured hands, divide and shape into about 65 small balls. Flatten each ball slightly.

5. Place the flattened dough balls on the baking sheets and sprinkle with the remaining allspice.

6. Bake in the preheated oven for 10–12 minutes, until crisp. Let cool on the baking sheets for 5 minutes, then transfer to a wire cooling rack and let cool completely.

Snowflake Gingerbread

1. Preheat the oven to 350°F. Grease three baking sheets.

2. Sift the flour, ginger, and baking soda in a bowl. Add the butter and rub into the flour mixture until the mixture resembles fine bread crumbs, then stir in the brown sugar.

3. In another bowl, beat together the egg and corn syrup with a fork. Pour this mixture into the flour mixture and mix to make a smooth dough, kneading lightly with your hands.

4. Roll the dough out on a lightly floured work surface to about ¼ inch thick and cut into shapes using a snowflake-shape cutter. Transfer the cookies to the prepared baking sheets.

5. Bake in the preheated oven for 10 minutes, until golden brown. Remove the cookies from the oven and let cool for 5 minutes before transferring with a spatula to a wire rack to cool completely.

6. Once the cookies are cool, mix together the confectioners' sugar and lemon juice until smooth and put into a pastry bag fitted with a small tip. Pipe snowflake shapes onto each cookie, using the icing. Let set for a few hours.

Makes 30

Ingredients
2¾ cups all-purpose flour, plus extra for dusting
1 tablespoon ground ginger
1 teaspoon baking soda
1 stick butter, softened, plus extra for greasing
¾ cup firmly packed dark brown sugar
1 egg, beaten
¼ cup light corn syrup

For the Decoration
1 cup confectioners' sugar
2 tablespoons lemon juice

Cookie Candy Canes

Makes 40

Ingredients

2¾ cups all-purpose flour,
   plus extra for dusting
1 teaspoon baking soda
1 stick butter, softened,
   plus extra for greasing
¾ cup firmly packed light
   brown sugar
1 egg, beaten
1 teaspoon vanilla extract
¼ cup light corn syrup

For the Decoration

3⅔ cups confectioners' sugar
½ cup lemon juice
red food coloring

1. Preheat the oven to 350°F. Grease three baking sheets.

2. Sift the flour and baking soda in a bowl. Add the butter and rub into the flour mixture until the mixture resembles fine bread crumbs, then stir in the brown sugar. In another bowl, beat together the egg, vanilla extract, and corn syrup with a fork. Pour this mixture into the flour blend and stir to make a smooth dough, kneading lightly with your hands.

3. Roll the dough out on a lightly floured work surface to about ¼ inch thick and cut into shapes, using a candy cane-shape cutter. Transfer the cookies to the prepared baking sheets. Bake in the preheated oven for 10 minutes, until golden brown. Remove the cookies from the oven and let cool for 5 minutes, before transferring, using a spatula, to a wire rack to cool completely.

4. Once the cookies are cool, mix together 2¼ cups of the confectioners' sugar and ⅓ cup of the lemon juice until smooth. Spoon the mixture into a pastry bag fitted with a fine tip and pipe the icing around the edge of the cookies. Empty any remaining icing into a small bowl, color it with the red food coloring, and cover with plastic wrap. Mix the remaining confectioners' sugar with the remaining lemon juice until smooth and runny. Spoon this into the center of each cookie and encourage it to the piped edge to flood each cookie. Let set overnight. Spoon the red icing into a pastry bag fitted with a fine tip and pipe stripes, dots, and swirls over the dry iced cookies.

Chocolate Covered Gingerbread

1. Put the butter, sugar, and corn syrup into a saucepan and heat gently, stirring all the time, until the butter has melted and the sugar has dissolved. Let cool for 10 minutes.

2. Sift the flour, ginger, allspice, and baking soda into a large bowl. Make a well in the center and pour in the melted mixture and beaten egg. Mix to a soft dough. Knead lightly until smooth, then wrap in plastic wrap and chill in the refrigerator for 30 minutes.

3. Preheat the oven to 350°F. Grease two large baking sheets.

4. Roll the dough out on a lightly floured surface to a ¼-inch thickness. Using a 2¾-inch round cookie cutter, stamp out 18 circles, rekneading and rerolling the dough as necessary. Place on the prepared baking sheets.

5. Bake in the preheated oven for 10 minutes, or until golden brown and just set. Let cool on the baking sheets for 2–3 minutes, then transfer to a wire rack to cool completely.

6. To decorate, dip the top of each gingerbread cookie in the melted semisweet chocolate to completely cover, then place on a wire rack. Spoon the melted milk chocolate into a paper pastry bag. Snip the end and pipe swirls or zigzags over the chocolate coated cookies. Let stand in a cool place until the chocolate has set.

Makes 18

Ingredients
6 tablespoons butter, diced, plus extra for greasing
½ cup firmly packed light brown sugar
2 tablespoons light corn syrup
2¼ cups all-purpose flour, plus extra for dusting
2 teaspoons ground ginger
½ teaspoon allspice
1 teaspoon baking soda
1 egg, lightly beaten
8 ounces semisweet chocolate, melted
2 ounces milk chocolate, melted

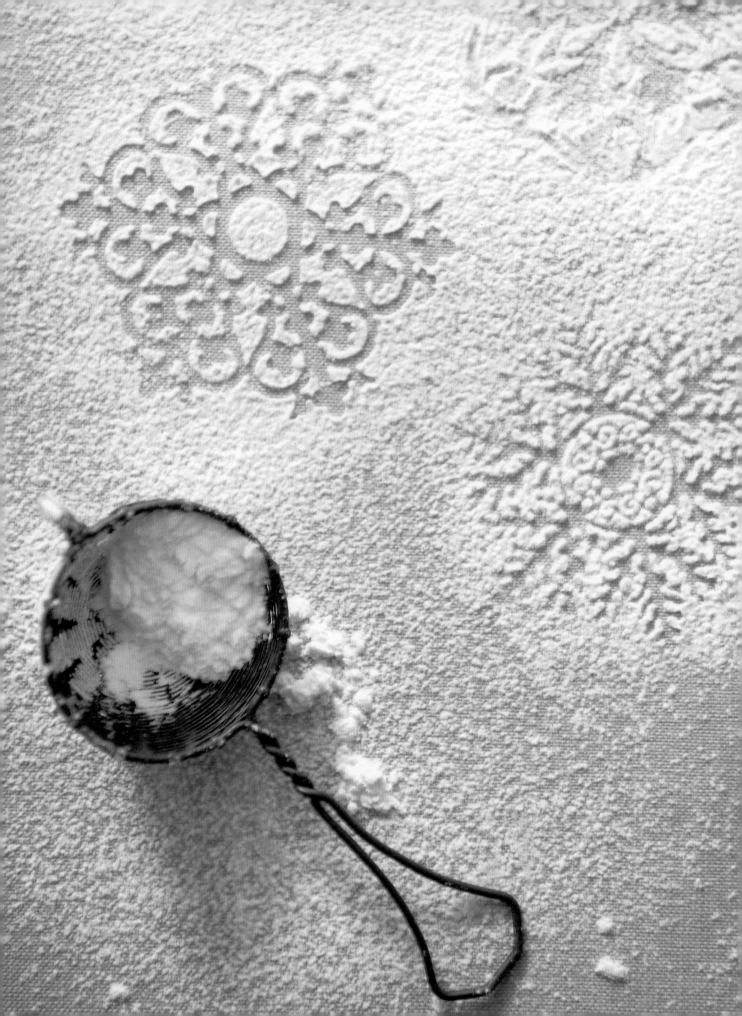

Cinnamon Stars

Makes 28

Ingredients
2 egg whites
¾ cup superfine sugar
2 teaspoons ground cinnamon
1¾ cups roasted hazelnuts,
    coarsely ground
1¾ cups ground almonds
    (almond meal)
3 tablespoons confectioners'
    sugar, plus extra for dusting

For the Icing
1 egg white
1⅔ cups confectioners' sugar,
    sifted
1-2 teaspoons lemon juice

1. Put the egg whites into a large bowl and, using a handheld electric mixer, beat until holding soft peaks. Gradually beat in the superfine sugar to make a firm glossy meringue mixture.

2. Fold in the cinnamon, ground hazelnuts, and almonds to make a firm, slightly sticky dough. Cover and chill in the refrigerator for 1 hour.

3. Preheat the oven to 300°F. Line two large baking sheets with parchment paper.

4. Sift half the confectioners' sugar onto a work surface. Add the dough and knead lightly until no longer sticky, sifting over more confectioners' sugar, if necessary.

5. Dust a rolling pin thickly with confectioners' sugar and roll the dough out to ½-inch thickness. Using a small star-shape cutter (about 2½ inches), stamp out stars and place on the prepared baking sheets. Reroll the dough as necessary, adding more confectioners' sugar to prevent it from sticking.

6. To make the icing, beat the egg white in a bowl and gradually beat in the confectioners' sugar until stiff. Beat in enough of the lemon juice to create a spreadable consistency. Using a small spatula, gently spread a little of the icing onto the top of each star.

7. Bake in the preheated oven for 15–20 minutes, until just set. Turn the oven off and leave the door ajar. Keep the baking sheets in the oven for 30 minutes. Transfer to a wire rack and let cool completely. Dust lightly with confectioners' sugar.

Christmas Tree Cookies

1. Sift the flour and spices into a bowl and rub in the butter until the mixture resembles bread crumbs. Add the honey and mix together well to form a soft dough. Wrap the dough in plastic wrap and chill in the refrigerator for 30 minutes.

2. Meanwhile, preheat the oven to 350°F and grease two baking sheets. Divide the dough in half. Roll out one piece of dough on a floured work surface to about ¼ inch thick. Cut out tree shapes using a cutter or cardboard template. Repeat with the remaining piece of dough.

3. Put the cookies on the prepared baking sheets and, using a toothpick, make a hole through the top of each cookie large enough to thread a ribbon through. Chill in the refrigerator for 15 minutes.

4. Bake in the preheated oven for 10–12 minutes, until golden brown. Let cool on the baking sheets for 5 minutes, then transfer to a wire rack to cool completely. Decorate the trees with white icing and colored balls, or simply leave them plain, then thread a length of ribbon through each hole and knot. Hang from the Christmas tree.

Makes 12

Ingredients
1¼ cups all-purpose flour,
   plus extra for dusting
1 teaspoon ground cinnamon
½ teaspoon ground nutmeg
½ teaspoon ground ginger
5 tablespoons unsalted butter,
   softened, plus extra
   for greasing
3 tablespoons honey

For the Decoration
white icing (optional)
edible colored balls

Chocolate Dominoes

Makes 16

Ingredients

1⅓ cups all-purpose flour
1½ teaspoons baking powder
¼ cup ground almonds
  (almond meal)
¾ cup granulated sugar
1½ sticks butter, softened,
  plus extra for greasing
3 extra-large eggs, lightly
  beaten
½ teaspoon almond extract
2 tablespoons seedless
  raspberry preserves
7 ounces marzipan
confectioners' sugar, for dusting

**For the Chocolate Icing &
Decoration**

6 ounces semisweet chocolate,
  broken into pieces
4 tablespoons unsalted butter
2 tablespoons light corn syrup
2 ounces white chocolate,
  melted

1. Preheat the oven to 350°F. Grease an 8-inch square cake pan and line the bottom with parchment paper.

2. Sift the flour and baking powder into a large bowl and add the ground almonds, granulated sugar, butter, eggs, and almond extract. Beat with an electric handheld mixer for 2–3 minutes, until thoroughly combined. Spoon the batter into the prepared cake pan and gently level the surface. Bake in the preheated oven for 35–40 minutes, or until golden brown, risen, and just firm to the touch. Let stand in the pan for 10 minutes, then turn out onto a wire rack and let cool completely.

3. Put the cake onto a board and, using a serrated knife, level the top of the cake, then spread with the preserves. Roll out the marzipan thinly on a surface lightly dusted with confectioners' sugar and trim to an 8-inch square. Gently place the square of marzipan on top of the cake and smooth flat with your hands. Cut the cake into 16 smaller square cakes. Place all the cakes on a board and put in the freezer for about 45 minutes, until just firm.

4. To make the chocolate icing, place the semisweet chocolate, butter, and syrup in a double boiler or a heatproof bowl set over a saucepan of simmering water. Heat until melted, then remove from the heat and stir until smooth. Let stand in a cool place for 30–40 minutes, stirring occasionally until the icing has thickened but still has a spoonable consistency.

5. Remove the cakes from the freezer. Push the tines of a fork into the bottom of one cake and, holding it over the bowl, spoon the chocolate icing liberally over the cake to coat the top and sides. Let the excess icing run back into the bowl. Carefully place on a wire rack. Repeat to coat the rest of the cakes with the icing. Spoon the melted white chocolate into a paper pastry bag and snip off the end with scissors. Pipe dots on the cakes to decorate. Let stand in a cool place until set.

Spiced Rum Cookies

Makes 18

Ingredients

- 1½ sticks unsalted butter, softened, plus extra for greasing
- ¾ cup packed dark brown sugar
- 1¾ cups all-purpose flour
- pinch of salt
- ½ teaspoon baking soda
- 1 teaspoon ground cinnamon
- ¼ teaspoon ground coriander
- ½ teaspoon ground nutmeg
- ¼ teaspoon ground cloves
- 2 tablespoons dark rum

1. Preheat the oven to 350°F. Grease two baking sheets.

2. Cream together the butter and sugar and beat until light and fluffy. Sift the flour, salt, baking soda, cinnamon, coriander, nutmeg, and cloves into the creamed mixture.

3. Stir the dark rum into the creamed mixture. Place 18 spoonfuls of the dough onto the prepared baking sheets, spaced well apart. Flatten each one slightly with the back of a spoon.

4. Bake in a preheated oven for 10–12 minutes, until golden brown. Let the cookies cool and crisp on wire racks before serving.

Cranberry & Coconut Cookies

Makes about 30

Ingredient
- 2 sticks butter, softened
- ¾ cup granulated sugar
- 1 egg yolk, lightly beaten
- 2 teaspoons vanilla extract
- 2¼ cups all-purpose flour
- pinch of salt
- ½ cup dry unsweetened coconut
- ½ cup dried cranberries

1. Preheat the oven to 375°F. Line two baking sheets with parchment paper.

2. Put the butter and sugar into a bowl and mix well with a wooden spoon, then beat in the egg yolk and vanilla extract. Sift the flour and salt into the mixture, add the coconut and cranberries, and stir until thoroughly combined. Scoop up tablespoons of the dough and place in mounds on the prepared baking sheets, spaced well apart.

3. Bake in the preheated oven for 12–15 minutes, until golden brown. Let cool on the baking sheets for 5–10 minutes, then, using a spatula, carefully transfer to wire racks to cool completely.

Christmas Macarons

1. Put the ground almonds, confectioners' sugar and allspice into a food processor and process for 15 seconds. Sift the mixture into a bowl. Line two baking sheets with wax paper.

2. Put the egg whites into a large bowl and beat until they hold soft peaks. Gradually beat in the superfine sugar to make a firm, glossy meringue. Using a spatula, fold the almond mixture into the meringue one-third at a time. When all the dry ingredients are thoroughly incorporated, continue to cut and fold the mixture until it forms a shiny batter with a thick, ribbonlike consistency.

3. Pour the batter into a pastry bag fitted with a ½-inch plain tip. Pipe 32 small mounds onto the prepared baking sheets. Tap the baking sheets firmly onto a work surface to remove air bubbles. Sprinkle half the macarons with the grated nutmeg and edible gold balls. Let stand at room temperature for 30 minutes. Meanwhile, preheat the oven to 325°F.

4. Bake in the preheated oven for 10–15 minutes. Cool for 10 minutes, then carefully peel the macarons off the wax paper. Let cool completely.

5. To make the filling, beat the butter and orange juice and rind in a bowl until fluffy. Gradually beat in the allspice and confectioners' sugar until smooth and creamy. Fold in the candied cherries. Use to sandwich together pairs of macarons.

Makes 16

Ingredients
¾ cup ground almonds
  (almond meal)
1 cup confectioners' sugar
1 teaspoon ground allspice
2 extra-large egg whites
¼ cup superfine sugar
½ teaspoon freshly grated
  nutmeg
1 teaspoon edible gold balls

For the Filling
4 tablespoons unsalted butter,
  softened
juice and finely grated rind of
  ½ orange
1 teaspoon ground allspice
1 cup confectioners' sugar,
  sifted
¼ cup candied cherries,
  finely chopped

Gingersnaps

Makes 30

Ingredients
2¾ cups all-purpose flour
2¾ teaspoons baking powder
pinch of salt
1 tablespoon ground ginger
1 teaspoon baking soda
1 cup granulated sugar
1 stick butter, plus extra
    for greasing
¼ cup light corn syrup
1 egg, beaten
1 teaspoon grated orange rind

1. Preheat the oven to 325°F. Lightly grease several baking sheets.

2. Sift the flour, baking powder, salt, ginger, and baking soda into a large mixing bowl and add the sugar.

3. Heat the butter and corn syrup in a saucepan over low heat until the butter has melted. Remove the pan from the heat and let cool slightly, then pour the contents onto the dry ingredients.

4. Add the egg and orange rind and mix thoroughly with a wooden spoon to form a dough. Using your hands, carefully shape the dough into 30 even balls. Place the balls on the prepared baking sheets, spaced well apart, then flatten them slightly with your fingers.

5. Bake in the preheated oven for 15–20 minutes, then carefully transfer to a wire rack to cool completely.

Oatmeal Cookies

1. Preheat the oven to 350°F and grease a large baking sheet.

2. Cream the butter and sugar together in a large mixing bowl. Beat in the egg, water, and vanilla extract until the mixture is smooth.

3. In a separate bowl, mix together the oats, flour, salt, and baking soda. Gradually stir the oat mixture into the creamed mixture until thoroughly combined.

4. Place well-spaced tablespoonfuls of the dough onto the prepared baking sheet. Bake in the preheated oven for 15 minutes, or until golden brown. Remove from the oven and cool on a wire rack.

Makes 15

Ingredients
1½ sticks butter or margarine,
* plus extra for greasing*
1⅓ cups raw brown sugar
1 egg
¼ cup water
1 teaspoon vanilla extract
4 cups rolled oats
1¼ cups all-purpose flour,
* sifted*
1 teaspoon salt
½ teaspoon baking soda

Jelly Swirls

Makes 20

Ingredients

2¾ cups all-purpose flour,
   plus extra for dusting
⅔ cup ground almonds
   (almond meal)
1¾ sticks cold butter,
   cut into small dice
½ cup granulated sugar
grated rind of a small orange
pinch of salt
2 eggs, lightly beaten
1 egg yolk
1 teaspoon vanilla extract
⅔ cup cherry or raspberry jelly
   or preserves
confectioners' sugar, for dusting

1. Sift the flour onto a work surface and sprinkle the ground almonds on top, along with the diced butter. Sprinkle with the granulated sugar, orange rind, and salt and mix well. Add the eggs, egg yolk, and vanilla extract and knead together to form a smooth dough. Wrap with plastic wrap and rest in the refrigerator for at least an hour.

2. Preheat the oven to 350°F. Line a baking sheet with parchment paper.

3. Turn the dough out onto a floured surface and roll it out to a thickness of ⅛ inch. Brush the excess flour away and use three pastry cutters with 2½-inch, 1¾-inch, and 1¼-inch diameters to cut out cookies. Use a ½-inch diameter cutter to cut out the center and create a ring from the smallest cookie. Place on the prepared baking sheet.

4. Bake in the preheated oven for about 12 minutes. Remove the rings after 8 minutes, because they will brown faster than the other cookies.

5. While the cookies are cooling, gently warm the jelly or preserves and pass through a fine strainer. Spread the jelly on the cookies and build the swirls up, finishing with the rings. Finally, dust with the confectioners' sugar to serve.

Reindeer Cookies

1. Crush the cardamom pods lightly in a mortar and pestle and discard the shells. Grind the cardamom seeds to a powder. Beat together the butter and granulated sugar in a bowl with an electric mixer until creamy, then gradually beat in the egg, orange rind, and cardamom powder.

2. Sift the flour, cornstarch, and baking powder into the mixture and stir with a wooden spoon to form a soft dough. Wrap the dough in plastic wrap and chill in the refrigerator for 30 minutes.

3. Preheat the oven to 350°F. Grease three baking sheets. Roll out the chilled dough on a lightly floured work surface to ⅛ inch thick. Cut out shapes using a reindeer-shape cutter, and place on the prepared baking sheets. Reknead and reroll the scraps and cut out more shapes until all the dough is used.

4. Bake in the preheated oven for 15 minutes, until just golden brown. Let cool for 5 minutes before transferring to a wire rack to cool completely.

5. Mix together the confectioners' sugar and lemon juice until smooth. Spoon 2 tablespoons of the mixture into a separate mixing bowl and color it with the red food coloring. Spoon the rest of the icing into a pastry bag fitted with a fine tip and pipe antlers, hooves, tail, collar, and a saddle in white icing on the cookies. Pipe a nose using the red icing. For the eye, attach a silver ball using a blob of icing.

Makes 25

Ingredients
10 cardamom pods
1 stick butter, softened,
 plus extra for greasing
¼ cup granulated sugar
1 egg, beaten
finely grated rind of ½ orange
1¾ cups all-purpose flour,
 plus extra for dusting
3 tablespoons cornstarch
½ teaspoon baking powder

For the Decoration
¾ cup confectioners' sugar
4 teaspoons lemon juice
red food coluring
25 edible silver balls

Sticky Ginger Cookies

Makes 20

Ingredients

2 sticks butter, softened
¾ cup granulated sugar
1 egg yolk, lightly beaten
3 tablespoons coarsely chopped
    preserved ginger, plus
    1 tablespoon syrup from
    the jar
2¼ cups all-purpose flour
pinch of salt
⅓ cup semisweet chocolate
    chips

1. Put the butter and sugar into a bowl and mix well with a wooden spoon, then beat in the egg yolk and ginger syrup. Sift together the flour and a pinch of salt into the mixture, add the preserved ginger and chocolate chips, and stir until thoroughly combined.

2. Shape the dough into a log, wrap in plastic wrap, and chill in the refrigerator for 30–60 minutes.

3. Preheat the oven to 375°F. Line two baking sheets with parchment paper.

4. Unwrap the log and cut it into ¼-inch slices with a sharp serrated knife. Put them on the prepared baking sheets, spaced well apart.

5. Bake in the preheated oven for 12–15 minutes, until golden brown. Let cool on the baking sheets for 5–10 minutes, then, using a spatula, carefully transfer the cookies to wire racks to cool completely.

Checkerboard Cookies

1. Put the butter and sugar into a bowl and mix well with a wooden spoon, then beat in the egg yolk and vanilla extract. Sift the flour and salt into the mixture and stir until thoroughly combined.

2. Divide the dough in half. Add the ginger and orange rind to one half and mix well. Shape the dough into a log 6 inches long. Flatten the sides and top to square off the log to 2 inches high. Wrap in plastic wrap and chill in the refrigerator for 30–60 minutes. Add the cocoa to the other half of the dough and mix well. Shape into a flattened log exactly the same size as the first one, wrap in plastic wrap, and chill in the refrigerator for 30–60 minutes.

3. Unwrap the dough and cut each flattened log horizontally into three slices. Cut each slice lengthwise into three strips. Brush the strips with egg white and stack them in threes, alternating the colors, so they are the same shape as the original logs. Wrap in plastic wrap and chill in the refrigerator for 30–60 minutes. Preheat the oven to 375°F. Line two baking sheets with parchment paper.

4. Unwrap the logs and cut into slices with a sharp serrated knife. Put the cookies on the prepared baking sheets, spaced well apart. Bake in the preheated oven for 12–15 minutes, until firm. Let cool for 5–10 minutes, then transfer to wire racks to cool completely.

Makes 20

Ingredients
2 sticks butter, softened
¾ cup granulated sugar
1 egg yolk, lightly beaten
2 teaspoons vanilla extract
2¼ cups all-purpose flour
pinch of salt
1 teaspoon ground ginger
1 tablespoon finely grated
  orange rind
1 tablespoon unsweetened
  cocoa powder, sifted
1 egg white, lightly beaten

Viennese Fingers

Makes about 16

Ingredients
1 stick unsalted butter,
  plus extra for greasing
2 tablespoons granulated sugar
½ teaspoon vanilla extract
¾ cup all-purpose flour
¾ teaspoon baking powder
4 ounces semisweet chocolate

1. Preheat the oven to 325°F. Lightly grease two baking sheets.

2. Put the butter, sugar, and vanilla extract into a bowl and cream together until pale and fluffy. Stir in the flour and baking powder, mixing evenly to a fairly stiff batter.

3. Put the batter into a pastry bag fitted with a large star tip and pipe about 16 fingers, each 2½ inches long, onto the prepared baking sheets.

4. Bake in the preheated oven for 10–15 minutes, until pale golden brown. Cool for 2–3 minutes on the baking sheets, then lift carefully onto a wire rack with a spatula to cool completely.

5. Place the chocolate in a double boiler or a small heatproof bowl set over a saucepan of gently simmering water until melted. Remove from the heat. Dip the ends of each cookie into the chocolate to coat, then place on a sheet of parchment paper and let set.

Almond Macarons

1. Preheat the oven to 350°F. Line two baking sheets with parchment paper.

2. Beat the egg white with a fork until frothy, then stir in the ground almonds, sugar, and almond extract, mixing to form a sticky dough.

3. Using lightly sugared hands, roll the dough into small balls and place on the prepared baking sheets. Press an almond half into the center of each.

4. Bake in the preheated oven for 15–20 minutes, or until pale golden brown. Place on a wire rack to cool.

Makes 12–14

Ingredients
1 egg white
1 cup ground almonds
   (almond meal)
⅓ cup superfine sugar,
   plus extra for rolling
½ teaspoon almond extract
6–7 blanched almonds,
   split in half

Gift Cookies

Makes 30

Ingredients

2 sticks butter, softened
¾ cup granulated sugar
1 egg yolk, lightly beaten
2 teaspoons orange juice or
  orange liqueur
finely grated rind of
  1 orange
2¼ cups all-purpose flour
pinch of salt

For the Decoration

1 egg white
1¾ cups confectioners' sugar
few drops each of 2 food
  colorings
edible silver balls

1. Put the butter and granulated sugar into a large bowl and beat together until pale and creamy, then beat in the egg yolk and orange juice and grated rind. Sift the flour and salt into the mixture and stir until combined. Halve the dough, shape into balls, wrap in plastic wrap, and chill in the refrigerator for 30–60 minutes.

2. Preheat the oven to 375°F. Line two large baking sheets with parchment paper. Unwrap the dough and roll out to ⅛ inch thick. Cut out star and holly shapes with cookie cutters and place them on the prepared baking sheets, spaced well apart. Bake in the preheated oven for 10–15 minutes, or until light golden brown.

3. Let cool on the baking sheets for 5–10 minutes, then transfer to wire racks to cool completely.

4. Put the egg white and confectioners' sugar into a bowl and beat until smooth, adding a little water, if necessary. Transfer half the icing to another bowl and color each bowl with a different color. Put both icings in pastry bags with fine tips and use to decorate the cookies, still on the wire racks, and write the initials of the person who will receive the cookies as a gift. Finish with silver balls and let set.

Index